I0561045

A. S. Morton

Beyond the palaeocrystic Sea

The Legend of Halfjord

A. S. Morton

Beyond the palaeocrystic Sea
The Legend of Halfjord

ISBN/EAN: 9783337151089

Printed in Europe, USA, Canada, Australia, Japan

Cover: Foto ©ninafisch / pixelio.de

More available books at **www.hansebooks.com**

Beyond the Palæocrystic Sea

or

The Legend of Halfjord

By A. S. MORTON

CHICAGO

PRIVATELY PRINTED

MDCCCXCV

INTRODUCTION

INTRODUCTION

My own story shall be as brief as possible, but it is necessary, to a complete understanding of how I came into possession of the facts given hereafter, that I should relate the circumstances surrounding my acquisition of the strange manuscript which follows.

In 1885 I was sent to Greenland by a scientific society that I might study and report on its geological structure, flora, fauna and all other matters of keen interest to the scientist, but of little value to the layman. Delighted at having secured the mission, for which I had unceasingly labored ever since the subject was broached, I lost no time in preparing for an absence of some years, and not many months after my appointment found myself located at Upernavik, one of the most northerly settlements of that inhospitable country.

3

With a species of intoxication I plunged at once into my work, being richly rewarded by the encomiums which reached me from my former fellow scientists in London, who seemed to fully appreciate my efforts and very kindly wrote to tell me so. These letters reached me only twice a year, both times during our brief Arctic summer, and the ships that bore them carried back my reports of months of earnest and untiring work.

Having, during two years of constant exploration and study, exhausted the territory lying about fifty miles north and the same distance south of my location, as well as penetrating the inland glacier itself, tramping many a weary mile over its frozen surface with no reward, since this great traveling ice wall presents on its moraineless face but few crumbs for the hungry scholar, I decided to press farther northward in search of new fields. Taking with me three of the hardy sons of that congealed race, I began my journey in November, 1887, choosing the winter, as it is not always comfortable to travel in those regions during their apology of a summer owing to the melting of the snow, which is the traveler's best friend. My first excursion was short and unproductive of results, but in February of the next year (1888) we set out again, this time equipped with a boat, as well as our sleds, and Upernavik saw us no more until the following autumn.

Enduring many hardships, we pressed steadily forward, my followers occasionally grumbling when, at times, 1 insisted upon remaining a day or two at some point where my harvest proved unexpectedly rich. Early in May we drew near Cape Parry and sighted the open water of Smith Sound; here we camped, it being my intention to remain some time. And while I explored the meagre footing of land, plucking here a flower, breaking off there a piece of rock, again studying some fossil generously offering itself to my eager eyes, my men spent most of their time on the water, bringing in an occasional fish or news of a whale, walrus, bear or fox sighted.

One evening (if an hour when the sun

should go down but obstinately refuses to do so can be termed evening) on my return to our quarters the men showed me a strangely shaped bag of walrus hide, tightly sewed with thongs of the same skin, which they had that day fished out of the water.

I examined it closely. It was smeared with tallow or blubber to make it water tight, and had evidently been prepared for a long stay in the water. Filled with the belief that within this bag was the history of the struggles and death of some of the heroes who have sought, at the price of their lives, to open up to the world this terra incognita, I handled it reverently as my knife cut the thongs. Within the bag was a roll of manuscript, or, more properly speaking, a parchment, since it was the dried and bleached skin of some animal. The closely written characters were very pale, but, to my delight, the writing was English, and I began at once to decipher it, working with a restless energy behind which were both curiosity and science.

That manuscript I give here, leaving the reader to do as he will with it. The scientist who desires scientific opinions may find them in my very lengthy and exhaustive report, rendered to the Society for Arctic Research, of London. This report has recently been published, and it will be found that I take therein the position that many of the statements made in this writing, so strangely cast into my hands, are hardly tenable in the light of even the little we know, and yet I am forced to admit that very many statements in the same writing are open to the unqualified approval and endorsement of every student of polar conditions, in addition to which, when I find myself still doubting, I ask myself where this manuscript could have come from if it is spurious, and then my mind reverts to the constantly recurring mirage seen off the coasts of Alaska—the vision of a strange city never yet found or identified, and I ask myself if it may not be that the story of this ice-walled man is true and the city of the Pole; that city never yet seen by us save in the skies.

THE MANUSCRIPT

THE MANUSCRIPT

I

My name is Pierre Vacheron ; I was born in New Orleans in 1820, am a Creole, and of good family. In 1845 I married Julie Ledere. (I pray she may now be living, and, if these pages ever reach that world I fear I shall never again see, I beg him who finds them to seek her and tell her of the fate which befell " Cher Pierre," as she always called me.)

We were very happy, Julie and I, but fortune frowned on us, and it was hard to see the dear one want for those things which ease the burdens of life. I sought other fields, hoping for better luck, and in 1850 we landed in Philadelphia. There I succeeded but indifferently, and the demon of restlessness, as well as of bitter discontent, entered my soul. Here the current of my

life changes, for in 1852 I met and became
very friendly with a man who I presume
made himself famous ; a man who, I
imagine, is even now reaping the fruits of
his heroism—Morton, who, on Kane's ex-
pedition, discovered the open arctic sea,
which up to that time none had seen.   He
visited me frequently.   Kane's expedition
was already the subject of much interest;
Morton was enthusiastic, I caught the con-
tagion.   Could it have well been otherwise
with my poor successes and constant rest-
lessness ?

The result of it all was that in 1853,
when Kane sailed in search of Franklin,
both Morton and Pierre Vacheron were
with him on board of the Advance.

It is not my intention to give any de-
tailed account of the expedition since, at
best, I can give but one side of it, and the
whole has doubtless long since been told
by those who, more fortunate than myself,
returned to their native land.   I shall but
refer to leading facts in order to show how
it is that I am now where I am.

We sailed in June, 1853, and in August

of that year reached Rensselaer Bay, and the last time I saw the brig Advance she was still there, and may be now so far as I know. That winter I was one of a party that, pushing north, reached very nearly the eightieth parallel, our journey being accompanied with terrible hardships, but safely accomplished. We were comparatively comfortable in our quarters on the ship, but Kane was indefatigable, working like a beaver himself, and sending us here, there, everywhere, to explore. I have lost track of many of my dates, but think it was about a year after our arrival when Morton led a party, of which I was a member, on the trip which should immortalize him, and doubtless has.

Our route lay up Kennedy Channel, opening from Smith Sound, and we pushed along until we had reached a latitude of more than eighty-one degrees north, when one day Morton suddenly gave a great shout, " The open polar sea !" pointing northward. All eyes at once turned in that direction, and there, sure enough, lay a vast expanse of open water stretching as

far as the eye could see. We were beside
ourselves with pride and delight. Each
man felt that he had made for himself an
undying name. I remember Morton con-
vulsively hugged me, and I think I hugged
him in return. At any rate, my naturally
volatile spirits were at high pressure just
then. A mad race started, I leading, over the
slippery slopes of the frozen wall surround-
ing this unfrozen sea. For hours I ran, think-
ing of nothing, unless it might be of dear
Julie and how proud she would be when I
returned. My companions, whom I had
long since distanced, were forgotten. In-
deed, myself and my own existence were
forgot as well. I think I was scarcely
human at the time, though the cause of this
sudden exhilaration I have never yet un-
derstood, being forced to content myself
with the belief that it was but the active
operation of that dread power known as
fate. Whatever may have been the cause,
I could not stop, nor indeed did the
thought of stopping enter my brain until
my body refused to longer bear the strain,
and I paused panting and breathless. I

seated myself on the ice, intending to rest until my companions came up, and, once seated, a thousand weird fancies came trooping through my brain as though I were bewitched. At last, being somewhat recuperated, I came to my senses and began to look around me. My first thought was one of uneasiness that my comrades had not come up, but I dismissed this idea, remembering how swiftly I had run, and tried to divert myself with the scene around me. This, however, did not serve to keep me long unconscious of my own loneliness. I soon became alarmed and, rising, sought to retrace my steps, when, what was my horror to see a wide expanse of water between myself and the land (or ice) I had left only a few hours before. I was adrift in this polar sea. Not a sign of life around me. I now was panic-stricken, paralyzed with fear, and shouted at the top of my voice, but no reply came save the mocking echo from the everlasting ice that rose around me like the frozen walls of a deserted hell.

For hours I shrieked like a madman,

hoping against hope, straining my eyes for a glimpse of those I had so shortly left, nor did I entirely relinquish hope until my observations showed me that I was steadily drifting north ; borne by a resistless current I was moving toward the unknown land of eternal ice, each gentle wave bearing me on from life and hope to death and despair. I felt that I was on my way to that Mecca of Arctic explorers, the Pole, and in my mind's eye could see my frozen body, laid out on this tomb of ice, circling around the globe's congealed axis, while my sight-less, staring eyes gazed ceaselessly up to that heaven whose splendor now mocked my impotent agony. Overcome with hope-less torture I fell in a swoon as deep as death save for its waking ; I know not how long I remained unconscious but it must have been for hours as, when I raised my-self and instinctively turned my gaze in the direction from which I had come, the ice wall which, so agonizingly far, had yet seemed so close, had grown dim in the distance and now loomed up against the horizon like the gloomy, fog-curtained banks of Newfoundland. I rose stiff with cold and, to rouse the circulation in my benumbed limbs as well as satisfy a mournful curiosity, began a tour of investigation, circling my icy tomb, which I judged to be about half a mile in circumference; the same sight greeted me at every turn—an unbroken expanse of water—desolation, death everywhere; my mind was tortured with varying scenes of agony; death from starvation, death from freezing, madness from overwhelming terror all grinned at me with their horrible faces so close to mine I felt as though their fetid breath fanned my cheeks. At one moment, in my paroxysms of impotent rage, I felt strong enough to strangle a polar bear, to cope with a famished lion; at another, shivering in every limb, I should have run in abject fear from even a titmouse. Time had lost its significance to me; having no way of noting the passage of day and night I could form no idea how long I had been on my awful cruise, but my next sensation was one of desperate hunger; in my frenzy I gnawed off great chunks of ice, devouring them only to find the same distressing emptiness ; I discovered imbedded in the ice a rock covered with a moss or lichen and this I tore off with greedy, trembling fingers, making of it a banquet fit for a king. My hunger somewhat appeased by this frugal repast, I gave more attention to things around me. The current to whose action I owed my uncomfortable situation was gently but resistlessly pushing, apparently, for the very Pole itself, bearing upon its placid bosom a living sacrifice. I knew I was beyond all human aid, and yet, such are the strange contradictions of human nature, I felt at that time a species of exaltation at the thought that I was the first rational creature to navigate this unknown sea and once or twice laughed hysterically as I thought of the novel bark upon which my voyage was undertaken. But then came, to interrupt this vagrant pleasantry, fear, desperation, the horrible gnawings of increasing hunger—my frame would collapse. I rolled on the ice in agony, almost hoping I would slip and roll off into the hungry waters, yet instinctively grasping any friendly projection. After awhile I grew impassive and lay awaiting the inevitable end, when my dull consciousness became impressed with the fact that the temperature was steadily rising and I remember my crazy fancies reverted to the ancient fables that the Pole was nothing but a great hole through which the waters unceasingly rushed but to be turned into steam by the unquenching fires beneath, and I thought this new warmth must be from the great volumes of steam and wondered how it must feel to be boiled, as I felt sure I was to be. At about this juncture a great white owl alighted on my bark and, settling comfortably down, sat solemnly blinking at me; in an instant the brute instinct fostered by hunger was alive within me. With a cunning born of insanity I drew close without disturbing or frightening him, seized him and with strength fed from the soul, seeing that the body was long since exhausted, held fast to my prey. He scratched and tore me but I wrung his neck and in a mad frenzy ripped him open with my knife, eagerly drinking his still warm blood. A life for a life—it seemed to me that each drop of this poor bird's blood as it trickled down my throat gave me a new lease on life. I felt once more the passion for life, that impulse which leads us to offer thanks unto the Creator that we are allowed to live, and with the thanks a prayer that we may be spared for further enjoyment of his gift of life. Hope's dying embers flashed up again into a flame whose intensity seemed to burn the walls of my breast within which its evanescent life was imprisoned. But man is a beast, an animal, at best, and my hunger was not appeased; I tore the feathers away and with my teeth dug great holes in the raw breast of the fowl, and, indeed, should probably have eaten the entire bird had I not remembered my situation and forced myself to put away the best part of it for future needs.

I was a man again! Such was the magic influence of that savage meal that I felt for a time absolutely safe and laughed at the chimerical fears of an hour before ; I even

went so far as to feel happy at the thought
that I was alone on this sea which mortal
man had never before traversed ; the Pole
had now no terrors for me; on the con-
trary, I longed for a speaking acquaintance
with this prime favorite of enthusiastic
scientists. But with returning vigor came
also the instinct of self-preservation, stifled
for a time by the paralyzation of life's
forces. Again and again I searched the
horizon closely but not a thing met my
eye save the ever-restless waters, an occa-
sional bird and a few floating islands of ice
similar to that which had so unceremoni-
ously abducted me.

From my condition when that ill-fated
owl fell into my hands I judge I must
have been afloat at least five days and, as I
roughly guess the speed of the current
bearing me to have been about thirty miles
a day, I conclude that I was then approxi-
mately 150 miles from my starting point
and, as well as I could judge in the absence
of any instruments, due north. I spent
my time watching with straining eyes for
any sign of life, any boundary to this

seemingly limitless sea ; but the last shred
of flesh had been torn from the bones of
my owl, and I was reduced to the necessity
of gnawing, dog-like, the bones themselves
before the dark outline of something other
than water marked the horizon.   When I
first saw this ragged fringe in the distance
I assumed that it was ice marking the limits
of the water, and I fell to speculating as to
whether we would impinge upon its frown-
ing wall, and either recoil, shattered, de-
stroyed, or remain welded to the mass, or
else, borne upon the wings of the silent
current, circle round and round this sea of
desolation for all time to come.   However,
I had not been long in sight of this bound-
ary before I saw that it could not be ice,
hence must be land, and no sooner did
this conviction force itself upon me than I
became fairly wild with joy.   If we could
only go close enough to that land for me
to leave my frozen craft I should feel
saved despite the fact that I was, at the
very least calculation, two hundred miles
from any human being and one thousand
miles from regular habitations.   I cannot

say that I had any idea of attempting to make my way back. Indeed, that would have been impossible, as I had not even so much as a compass, but I did have a very fixed idea of the desirability of maintaining my own animal life even under such discouraging circumstances, and it was this instinct of self-preservation which caused me to sound a note of triumph on the discovery of land. I felt like the buffeted mariner who, after barely escaping shipwreck, sees his port ahead of him. I have already alluded to the fact that the farther north I got the higher the temperature — for more than a day, as well as I could mark time, it would have been really too warm for my dress had it not been for the effect of the ice on which I floated; in fact, before I sighted land a new cause of alarm had arisen, as I had noticed a sensible diminution in the floe on which I rode. But now fear was cast aside; there to my right (northeast of Smith Sound as well as I could determine) lay land ; rugged and barren land, apparently, but land ; ice-bound and desolate, but still land ; doubt·

less refusing support of life to the few
birds that visited its untrod shores, yet it
might, nay, should, support and keep me;
it was land and in that one word I read
life, hope, safety. I quite forgot in my
excitement that I was again growing very
hungry; but one central idea held posses-
sion of my brain — that land and my
chances of reaching it. For hours I stead-
ily watched it, and gradually the strange,
ragged looking peaks took definite shape.
I grew more deeply interested; nearer still
— I rubbed my eyes and began to fear that
I had grown crazy — no, I was surely ra-
tional, yet could it be? I pinched myself
to make sure that I did not sleep — I was
awake. All the time I kept my eyes fixed
upon that distant shore, scarcely daring
even to wink for fear the dream, the mir-
age, the feverish fancy of a frenzied brain,
whichever it might be, would melt before
my gaze. I was sure that I had full pos-
session of all my faculties and yet equally
sure that the scene before me was an in-
substantial pageant born of the vaporings
of a too diseased brain. Rising in the

distance and slowly assuming tangible out-
lines rose in unmistakable clearness from
the unsounded depths of the sea, from the
unscaled heights of virgin peaks, a city,
yes, a city whose walls, towers, streets, be-
spoke not the hand of the Creator of all
things but the handiwork of man. What
was before me? If my eyes served me no
trick and this was really a city, was it a
city of the dead? of a people long since
perished? Was I doomed to wander a soli-
tary mortal through those silent streets,
finally to lie down and die as they who
reared those walls had died, within some
one of their deserted homes? I shuddered
at these thoughts. Had I entered the land
of magic, the home of the black art, and
had this great pile been reared by some
demon to torment and destroy me? These
and many other wild fancies chased one
another in wanton confusion through my
clouded brain while I steadily bore my
way, guided by some unseen hand, to-
ward the coast whose present aspect fright-
ened me far more than would have done
beetling cliffs fit for but the habitations of

feathery nomads. My sensations may possibly be faintly imagined, but no one who has not himself been an actor in such a drama can realize the terror, the superstitious despair that filled my soul. My limbs shook, I trembled all over and, unable to stand, sank in impotent paralysis of fear upon the ice. To my now crazed brain the breeze playing around me seemed the heated breath of a myriad of hellish imps, shrivelling my cheeks as it fanned them. The steady, irresistible movement of the dissolving ice relentlessly bearing me to frightful death, to annihilation, was to me but the work of some hidden devil who, in hideous glee disporting himself, was dragging me on and on that I might be offered a vicarious sacrifice to the arch-demon himself. The minutes seemed hours and yet I neared that uncanny city with what seemed to me frightful velocity. I had given myself up for lost from the moment when I found myself drifting, but now felt that I was damned in soul as well as body and would gladly have given my life for the privilege of dying among my fellow-men.

The strongest mind wavers under pressure, the bravest heart has its sudden leaps of fear, is it any wonder that I, with the spectacle of a completely equipped city here within a few miles of the Pole, apparent life amid eternal death, should have succumbed to the effect of the rude shock, especially considering my previous condition and the fearful strain I had borne? I think not, and while I now laugh at my agonizing fears, I have never been ashamed of them, though I may add, by way of parenthesis, that I am not what men call a coward.

Drifting, drifting, with not a star of hope in the glaring sky whose unblinking eye seemed to have forgot to sleep; nor anchor to hold, nor rudder to steer as I ploughed my way through the cold waves green with envious desire as they licked away, piece by piece, the glistening throne upon which sat in mock dignity one of creation's kings. Above me the heavens, illimitable, illuminated by the cold and ghastly glare of a sleepless sun; below the softly surging, silent sea whose whispering waves, caressing, creep through ever growing gaps upon my frozen craft, the while with restful restlessness, with the rare rhythm of their siren songs they bear me, helpless, hopeless, to *their* goal, *my* grave; beyond, the bare and barren ragged rocks against whose frowning face, with frightful force, I might be dashed or, those rocks escaped, that city of the dead, whose winding walls did mark the tortuous trail of the con-demned and tortured soul, its silent streets and hearthless homes the hopelessness of hell; its towering domes of demon make but fingers of fate, pointing upward, do show the way below to the noisome, bot-tomless depths of hell.

Nearer, still nearer, that silent current bore me.   I saw I should miss the rocks, yet seeing this saw, but too well, that I must ground upon the beach before that awful city, and in this knowledge found more of dread than of comfort.   Nearer, yet nearer — what is that I see?   Have the imps of hell taken tangible shape before my eyes?   Oh! Horror of horrors! They run in wanton glee to see the death of the body, the damnation of the soul! There they crowd before hell's open portal, that beach, and elbow and jostle one another that they may see my doom. More, still more of them, the shore is black with hell's minions. I even fancy I can hear their wicked shrieks of fiendish delight — my brain reels, something seems to crack with a snap within my head; mortal man can bear no more; in a senseless swoon I fall prone upon the ice, murmuring with my last fleeting consciousness a prayer to the Almighty.

I did not fall into the hands of imps, devils or goblins, but, what is still stranger to me, when I recovered from my swoon found myself in the hands of men. To my eyes they were strange and uncouth looking, but they were none the less men and seemingly mild and kind in disposition. I no sooner found myself safe from immediate danger of death than I became frantically hungry and at once essayed to make this fact known, but my captors were apparently rather dull and slow of wit, and it was only when I had about exhausted all signs known to me that they seemed to comprehend ; there was then great jabbering and gesticulating among them, when finally one who had seemed to bear the air of a dictator came forward (they had all been standing at a respectful distance from me) and, after first prostrating himself upon his face, waved his hand toward the city as though to invite me to enter its walls. Having already gathered that I was in good favor with my odd-looking hosts, and assuming that the road to food was the path leading into the city, I drew myself up and with as much dignity as my stiff and tottering limbs would support began my triumphal march, for such it proved to be. No sooner had I taken one step than the entire multitude fell face down prone upon the ground, and I really think they would have permitted me to tread upon them, since they never moved as I made my way with difficulty between them, rising only after I had passed and following at a respectful distance.

A great wall surrounded the city and when I entered its open gate a tremendous noise arose; it proved to be their music, consisting of drums made of walrus-hide stretched on frames and several wind instruments contrived chiefly out of the bones of birds. At the sound of this noise or music those remaining in the city, principally women and children, rushed

forth from their houses into the streets;
he who had silently invited me to be their
guest walked some distance ahead of me
crying certain strange words at sound of
which all who looked on prostrated them-
selves in silence until I had passed, when
they took up the same cry until the welkin
rang. Despite hunger, fatigue and sore-
ness the novelty of my position, the
strangeness of the people and the welcome
I received at their hands deeply impressed
me and I endeavored to walk with the air
of a mighty conqueror, though I fear with
poor success. For some distance I passed
through narrow streets lined on either side
with small stone houses, when finally my
leader paused in a square court and with a
profound obeisance indicated that I should
precede him into a large building whose
four towers I had so clearly seen while
floating toward this haven.

I entered as he bade me and immedi-
ately concluded that I was in their temple,
but soon began to doubt this when at the
farthest extremity of the edifice I came to
a great throne chiseled out of stone and

garnished with walrus tusks and similar trophies of the chase. Obedient to a silent gesture from my guide I mounted the throne and at the moment when I seated myself there was a great burst of their uncouth music, a shout from the people who had crowded after me into the building, and my eyes surveyed a vast sea of bowed heads; doubtless they would have again prostrated themselves had they not been too closely wedged. Food was now brought me, which I greedily devoured while the assembled multitude gazed in rapt attention; having stifled the pangs of hunger I felt the need of rest—I grew dull and heavy, my peaceful conquest of this unknown people interested me no longer, and I made desperate efforts to convey my wishes to the master of ceremonies, finally succeeding after I had cursed his stupidity in every language but his own. My wish was law. He spoke, the hum of the crowd hushed and as silently as the unreal shapes of a dream the vast crowd glided out; when the place was empty he led me to a corner where was a bed made of mosses and seaweed; upon this I threw myself, nor had mortal man ever softer couch.

I woke from my deep sleep refreshed but sorely perplexed and rubbed my eyes to assure myself that the events I have just related were no dream. But the reality of my surroundings was soon made apparent since no sooner did I stir than I was waited on with food and drink, the word was given outside, the people again poured into the temple, and again I seated myself on the throne and received what was evidently the worship of this race.

Having no means of measuring time I am unable to say how long this pantomime lasted, but, feeling that I should have to spend my days here, I immediately set to work to learn the language and soon succeeded reasonably well in understanding most of what was said, though I fear I shall never be able to pronounce a large proportion of their ear-splitting, jaw-breaking words, hence shall always prove a better listener than talker. I had assumed from the first that they had made me

either their prince or their god ; I now
found that I held the dual position. Half-
jord, their first king, according to their
legends, was also their god and they had a
fixed belief that he would some day return,
make of this barren waste a smiling gar-
den and of them a great and powerful peo-
ple ; when they saw me floating to them
on my ship of ice, coming from where
mortal had never before come so far as
they knew, they welcomed me as the long-
expected Halfjord, seated me upon that
throne which had for centuries awaited
him, and patiently waited to hear from my
lips what was to be the outcome. This in
brief was what I gathered with my first
understanding of their speech. I did not
find it convenient to disabuse their minds
of this harmless superstition, since it was
entirely to my advantage ; on the contrary,
I fostered their belief in my supernatural
attributes as far as I thought proper and
confess I revelled in the thought of being
an accepted king, even of this simple, un-
taught people.

Here I was, then, king of an unknown

race, god of an untaught people, spending my days in an unsought, unexplored coun- try.

Having now through means of this writing located myself, with the hope that some one may find my story and seek to restore me to my home and people, I shall devote but little time to describing those with whom my lot is cast, as I live with an ever-present hope—that of rescue—and writing is a thankless task when one's pa- per is the tanned skins of birds, pen a stick and ink the juice of an Arctic plant. Those who come to seek me can tell the world more of these strange people than, with my present opportunities, I am in- clined to tell. I shall, however, give a brief sketch of them but, before beginning, let me say a word to my rescuers, whom I now confidently expect, since I shall con- sign this history of mine to the same cur- rent which bore me hither and which I am sure must at some point north of us (per- haps at the Pole itself) turn and work itself south ; therefore I shall cast this, my story, upon the placid bosom of our im-

prisoned sea with serene confidence that it
will some day be found — heaven grant
that day be not too distant!

I have no instruments, consequently can
give no exact bearings, but if the search-
ing party will pass through Smith Sound
and up Kennedy Channel until they come
in sight of this open sea, and then bear
almost due west through the thousand
channels cutting into the ice, they will, in
about a day's journey, reach this polar cur-
rent, when all they have to do is to allow
it to bear them with it north-northeast to
this port. May the God of our race incline
the hearts of heroic men to brave the dan-
gers of the palæocrystic sea for my restor-
ation to home, friends, wife! Heaven
hear my prayer and bear this letter on the
bosom of the restless sea with lightning
speed to the land of my own people!

These people are undoubtedly of Scandinavian origin, and from their legends it would appear that the settlement was founded in about the year 900 by the Norsemen, those hardy, restless wanderers who made both history and nations. But none of the old spirit of adventure is left in these simple, childish folk; they seem contented with what they have, barring the one exception of their undying hope of Halfjord's return. They have no traditions, no legends beyond the life, adventures and death of this, their first king. Their simple, inoffensive disposition is doubtless due to force of circumstances, travel by land beyond a few miles being out of the question and travel by water equally impossible, owing to the absence of timbers for vessels. I have used every effort to induce them to build a great boat

of skins and let me lead an expedition of
discovery with the hope that I might thus
escape, but they will not hear of this, even
though I tell them it is necessary in order
that their resurrected Halfjord may do
those things of which they dream. It is
evident that they fear to have me leave
them even for a short time, and I am so
beset with attention, so closely followed at
all times, that independent escape, even if
I had the means of transportation, would
be entirely out of the question; in other
words, though enjoying the privileges of a
sovereign and the power of a deity, I have
always felt that I was a prisoner whose
every move was closely watched, my per-
son jealously guarded by my subjects; I
have no hope of escape and must live and
die their king, their god, unless my fellow-
men shall rescue me from this living death.

They are a simple people, as I have said
before—free from vices, kind and charita-
ble, hardy yet lacking in courage, cool
under circumstances where civilized (?)
man would be frantic with rage, but panic-
stricken when confronted with physical

danger ; in some senses ingenious but very primitive in their methods, though this may be accounted for by the fact that they really have nothing with which to work save iron and stone, both of which are found in great abundance. There are no trees, a few bushes and stunted pines, seldom reaching the height of a man's head, being all of the forest growth found here ; these they use solely for kindling fires, which are afterward fed by a lignite coal, of which great seams appear, even raising their grimy faces above the thin and poverty-stricken soil. It had never occurred to them to use this wood in any other way, and, when I showed them how to fasten a knife upon a pine staff and cast this weapon, javelin-like, at their chase, instead of, as they had been taught, stealing upon the prey and knifing it at close quarters, they regarded it as a miracle and proclaimed anew all through the city that I was indeed Halfjord; the young men watched me closely and soon became very proficient in the use of this their new weapon.

I said my subjects were free from vices,

and this is true looking at it from their standpoint, but it must be confessed that their views and customs regarding marriage are startling, to put it mildly; in fact, they really have no such thing as a marriage ceremony, nor do their laws or customs require but a single mate; there is frequently seen plurality of wives in some cases, husbands in others, but the relations between these parties last only so long as they are mutually agreeable, any or either of them being at perfect liberty to select other companions without prejudice. Strange to say, this freedom does not seem to be abused. Both polygamy and polyandry are commonly practiced, but what we would term divorces are infrequent, and in both cases the dual wives or husbands seem to live in perfect amity and content; it therefore follows that some of the most repulsive vices of civilization are unknown, though, as a natural consequence of their habits of life, these people have no conception of life's greatest blessing—the love of two united hearts wedded in perfect union. I have made some efforts in the direction of establishing a fixed marriage law, but mine are a stiff-necked people and ill brook interference with their settled institutions, even when that interference comes from him they worship, and I found my proposed measures so extremely unpopular that it seemed but the part of prudence to abandon for the present, at any rate, my attempt to establish monogamy.

I remember, when I woke from the heavy sleep just after my arrival, the leader (whom I afterward learned had been their prince until I appeared), with a great show of ceremony, presented twelve comely maidens, who thereafter attended me so closely as to frequently embarrass, even sleeping upon beds of moss laid in the same chamber as mine, though that could hardly be helped seeing that no house in the city possessed more than one chamber. At first I thought these young women were servants, but on gaining some familiarity with their language found they were my wives, had been tendered as such, and my tacit acceptance had completed the ceremony which bound them to me. How was

I to do otherwise than accept them when I knew not a word that was being said, nor how to decline so many brides? Somewhat disturbed by the information that I had unintentionally become a much married man I yet exercised the right belonging to me under the laws of Nikiva, and at once divorced the entire dozen — much to their regret, I fear, as they had seemed much elated at being wives of the great Halfjord. Under other circumstances I might have acted differently, but with the constantly recurring hope of rescue and the ever-present memory of my darling Julie waiting to welcome me I could not form any entangling alliances.

In stature my people are short, rather dwarfed and thick-set. (My people! How soon one falls into the habit of claiming a right of which he never dreamed until it was forced upon him.) Their complexions are clear, their coloring usually blonde — occasionally one sees a brunette — but red hair marks a child of the demon, and no sooner does a poor babe show on its bald pate a few red hairs than it is brought to the temple and there, before the assembled people, boiled alive; its flesh is then thrown into the sea, its bones afterward burned, and the water in which it was boiled poured over the house in which the child was born. I have tried to stop this barbarous custom, but they tell me it prevailed in Halfjord's time and, for fear of displaying, even to their dull wits, my unwitting imposture, and being possibly forced to submit to the inconvenience of being myself boiled, I keep quiet, after having entered a mild protest and met with vigorous opposition.

The climate here is wonderfully temperate. Summer lasts about three months, and during that time I should say our average temperature is about sixty degrees, while, judging from my own feelings, I think in mid-winter it has never been colder than twenty or thirty below, though we have a great deal of snow, which the natives get over by using sleds, ingeniously contrived of iron frames over which skins are stretched. Furs are seldom worn, the people dressing chiefly in skins from which the hair has been scraped, but in winter they wear an under-garment woven from a fibrous sea-plant or, in a few cases, made from the breast of the eider-duck.

Our food is principally flesh, sometimes fresh, usually dried. For birds we have the duck, ptarmigan and owl, the latter being considered quite a delicacy; our principal fish is the cod and among animals both the walrus and the wolf are deemed choice morsels; the whale is sometimes seen but not sought after by these people, who have no taste for the blubber which forms so important a part of the diet of the Esquimax further south. One vegetable is raised here but I cannot well describe it as I know of nothing to which to compare it. I rather incline to the belief that it is a cross between the potato and the turnip; it is nauseating at first but one grows to like it and the natives consider it a great luxury. I may say in passing that my stomach has not entirely accustomed itself to the radical change and I frequently pine for a good beefsteak and some bread, both of which are, of course, unknown in this semi-barbarous, wholly abandoned land.

I have already told of the mild inoffensiveness of the people and in support of this I find that there is record of but one murder since the founding of the city of Nikiva; the culprit was boiled (their usual mode of exorcising the devil), and his bones are still exhibited in the temple which is my abiding place — a palace, sanctuary and charnel-house at one and the same time.

I am writing as I get the opportunity, and under many disadvantages; among them the curiosity of the people who, having never seen writing, think I am dealing in magic and, while they fully expect that from Halfjord, yet are consumed with curiosity as to the marks I make and pester the life out of me. Hence, I presume I have put down many things that need explanation, but I hardly feel like explaining them. In truth, I am giving only skeleton information, as I hope some day to welcome men from my own country who will take me back and with me a more complete description of this forgotten land, but I remember one statement that I must at least qualify—it is regarding the absence of vice; the vice of drunkenness exists here and I might say not even the babe in the arms is free from it, but as it occurs only on special occasions it might be charitable to overlook it, after all. The Nikivans distill a powerful stimulant from the juice of their stunted pines, mixed with a pulp from the leaves of a shrub known as "org," this drink they call "nogalik" and the entire populace busy themselves preparing it each summer when the sap runs, storing it in walrus-hide casks(?). It must not be inferred, however, that this liquor is promiscuously drunk; on the contrary, it is carefully put aside and makes its appearance only when the grim reaper, Death, comes to Nikiva. On such occasions the entire populace repair to the temple, where the body lies stretched upon an iron frame, and there for a space of time which I should judge to be about two days they give themselves up to orgies beside which an ordinary Irish wake pales into insignificance, save that the former is always good natured, the latter sometimes a bit rough, as I distinctly remember from my own experience at one. At our wakes here the very first duty of every good citizen, male or female, is to get gloriously drunk, and to this end are copious libations of "nogalik" served; one by one the crowd becomes first noisy, then hilarious, then stupid, and as the latter stage comes on they fall where they are and sleep it off. This performance is repeated three times and, after arousing from the third drunken stupor, they bear the body to the beach and toss it into the water. Should an epidemic visit us I very much fear me Nikiva would get so drunk as never to be able to sober up again, but as it is now, so soon as the body is cast into the water, Nikiva returns to its usual irreproachable sobriety, repeating the orgy only when another unfortunate bids adieu to this mundane sphere.

Of religion we have none save the worship of Halfjord, now become the worship of myself as Halfjord returned. The prince or ruler is also priest and it has been his

mission to preach to the people the return
of the long expected restorer, hence I now
find myself in the equivocal position of
preaching myself as their messiah returned
to lead them to glory, power, happiness.
I cannot say that I relish this self-stultifi-
cation, but man will do much for life—
will inflict mortal injury upon that eternal
thing known as the soul for the sake of
that insignificant phosphorescent flash
called life, and I seem to be no excep-
tion to the rule; I daily preach myself to
these ignorant people and when my con-
science upbraids me stifle it with the
thought that if I told them the truth they
would not believe me, or, if believing, they
killed me as an impostor, they would still
continue to worship and look for the re-
turn of their Halfjord. With this view of
the case I do not find it hard to persuade
myself that I am preserving the life God
gave me and at the same time doing no
harm to any one, not even myself; I go
even farther than this, assuming with su-
preme self-complacency that with my ad-
vanced and civilized ideas I may be able

to help these people, lifting them up to a higher plane, arguing with specious sophistry that the greatest good of the greatest number demands some self-sacrifice on my part. But it is not worth while to spend time explaining my motives; every man has been through very much the same experience at some time in his life and if there be a man so fortunate as never to have been forced to the use of trumped-up arguments for the justification of his own course, yet is even he sufficiently aware of humanity's weakness to need no lengthy dissertation from me. I did it—I still persist in the same course of action—I do not believe I have shown more moral turpitude than the average man.

My brief account of the people over whom I am now supreme ruler is ended when I say that my great nation consists of about eighty thousand souls; now be it my task to find a fitting opportunity for consigning to the waves this prayer for succor, this greeting to my poor little wife, who has doubtless long since given me up for lost; this appeal to the land of light for one flash to break the impenetrable gloom of this everlasting darkness.

My watchers are very jealous of my movements, and I may find it troublesome to get rid of this now that I have written it, since they have already shown a decided inclination to take unto themselves these sheets, of whose mysterious cabalistic characters they have no understanding. They have given me to know that they consider this scratching of mine closely allied with their destiny and mine, and do not propose to lose sight of it any more than of me. I am required to deposit it with a keeper chosen by the people whenever I weary of writing, and receive it from his hands when I wish to resume my narrative. For the present, at least, my case seems hopeless; may the God of mercy soften their hearts and grant a fair voyage to my message.

1860.

My dates are, of course, haphazard, being based entirely on the passage of the seasons, and I know not if I am right as to the year, either now or before, but twice

have the seasons rolled around since I
wrote the last word above, and still I have
been unable to elude the vigilance of these
people and send my message on its solitary
journey.

My poor Julie, doubtless you have long
since donned a widow's weeds and wept in
silence over the unknown fate of your
Pierre; I will not insult your faithful heart
by dreaming that, listening to whispered
words from other lips, you have allowed
the noisome weeds of sorrow to blossom
once more into the rose of love and given
your heart to another. Poor child, in my
suffering I ceaselessly remember you alone
with your grief, shut up in a heart too ten-
der for the rude laceration of such sorrow.
Merciful God! If *I* have no claim upon
Thy mercy at least *she* has, pure as the
driven snow, sinless, sanctified; for her sake
I pray Thee bear my message safely on the
bosom of this unfathomable ocean.

My people have begun to grow restless
for the glory and power Halfjord was to
bring them and I have finally succeeded
in cajoling them into the belief that it is

necessary to the full consummation of their expectations that this manuscript be sent on its journey, and have assured them that after the lapse of four recurring sets of seasons (four years as we would say) an answer shall come, that answer being the beginning of the fulfillment of their prophecies.

The time is at hand, the walrus-hide is ready to receive my message, I but add a word before trusting my all to the mercy of yonder waves. I say all my hopes, because these people, inoffensive as they are naturally, bear no trifling, and if, by the expiration of the time I have set, I am not rescued, the boiling-pot with all its horrors stares me in the face. The consignment of my writing to the sea is to be made a public ceremony. The people are already moving toward the shore to the strains of their unearthly music, and in a moment I must join them, and, with a smile on my lips, agony in my heart, cast my last die.

During the long wait since I finished the story of my wanderings I have gathered into compact form the legend of

Halfjord, and to while away tedious hours have woven it into a romance. I enclose the whole along with this, my prayer for succor. It may reach that which I term the world too late to be of any service to me, in which case I bequeath it to my dear wife, Julie Vacheron, of Philadelphia.

One prayer more and I have done : O! Thou God who holdest in the hollow of Thy hand this universe, I beseech Thee look in pity upon Thy unworthy servant, doomed to a life but little better than that hell Thou hast ordained for sinners! If I have found favor in Thy sight I beseech Thee succor me in this my hour of need! If, O, Lord, I am too great a sinner for Thy tender mercies even then I pray Thee, O God, spare me that I may learn to walk in the paths of righteousness. Spare me, O God! for the sake of her who hath given her life unto Thee and who loveth me. Spare me, heavenly Father!

I now place myself in God's hands.

PIERRE VACHERON.

THE LEGEND OF HALFJORD

THE LEGEND OF HALFJORD

CHAPTER I

The good king Halfjord had gathered
his knights and gentlemen and for the
space of three days and nights great rev-
elry had reigned at his castle; from all
points of his kingdom his vassals had
hastened at his bidding, bringing with
them their ladies and a mighty following
of servants and men-at-arms. They had
come to pay homage unto their queen,
Halfjord's bride, the fair Grunhilde, and
surely vassal never bent the knee to love-
lier queen, nor did queen ever mate with
nobler consort. Thus it was that there
was great rejoicing. Valiant men and
noble dames passed the hours in the sweet
pleasantries of love's ever-changing fancies;
hardy hunters sought the savage boar in
his wild lair; lowly serfs drank the health
of their new mistress in generous draughts

drawn from the king's cellars; love and joy reigned supreme and life was like a summer morn. But, alas ! all things end, the rosiest dream has its waking, and Death's hideous spectre stalks ever in advance of all earthly pageants.

It was about noon of the fourth day. Halfjord and his nobles with their retainers were off to the chase; the women, left alone, busied themselves as only women can, each with her thoughts filled with some gallant squire whose sword and lance were ever at his king's service. There was the clatter of hoofs in the courtyard, a hurried movement among the waiting menials, the sound of steps, and, following close upon the heels of the maid who announced him, entered a young man. Tall, magnificently formed, his curling locks blowing carelessly in the wind, his drooping moustache seeking to hide the too severe lines of a mouth formed but for determination, he was a fine sight even though covered with dust from his long ride.

As he entered the queen looked up and

spoke in rather playful chiding: "Ah! Olaf, our festivities were not complete without you. Methinks you are tardy in paying homage to your queen." The young man, first casting his eye on a maiden who, with flushed cheek and heaving breast, sought to conceal her furtive glances, approached close to the queen, and, bending his knee, said, "Fair queen, it needeth not Olaf's presence to prove his devotion; my duty to my sovereign king has kept me from the festive board; that same duty brings me first to thy feet on my return. I would fain have made one of the merry party that first offered thee homage, but sterner tasks have kept me from thy presence; if I live I hope to prove to thee that thou hast no more loyal subject than Olaf." Stooping still lower he kissed the queen's outstretched hand, adding, "Accept, I pray thee, my homage, fair queen. Though tardy it hath behind it the true and loyal heart of a devoted subject."

Grunhilde smiled. "Methinks," she graciously said, "our liege lord, Halfjord,

hath a tried and faithful servant in you.
But while we wait return of our lords
from the heated chase, beguile the weary
hours with story of your adventures; truly,
these maids and wives weary of their tapes-
try, and would fain hear from noble lips
the tale of manly deeds. What duty kept
Olaf so long from feet of his queen,
and whence come you spurring so hotly
that the dust of the road lieth on you even
as thick as the snows of winter? What
news bringeth Olaf ?"

The young man seemed distressed at
her questionings, and a covert glance at
the maid on whom his eyes had first rested
discovered her eagerly waiting his reply.
He hesitated. An imperious gesture from
the queen bade him speak. "Nay, fair
queen," he faltered, "what hath Grun-
hilde with stern affairs of state that call
for scheming brains and iron hands?
Thou hast thy king, most valiant of men ;
thy kingdom, fairest spot on this earth ;
thy subjects, faithful and true ; that were
enough. I pray thee disturb not thy
dainty mind, nor wrinkle thy sweet face

with secrets of state that do too frequent
prove a weight so heavy even the strongest
mind droppeth or betrayeth them. Live
thou, O, queen, in the rosy bowers of
youth and love while yet thou hast them
within thy grasp, nor seek to destroy life's
sweetest flowers by plucking with too rude
a hand the gaily colored bloom of ambi-
tion's vine that withers in the grasp."

"Strange words these from subject to
queen," said Grunhilde in reply; "stranger
still when I bethink me you have not the
silvered hair of the sage, grown gray in
service of his king ; nay, your years are
no greater than mine, and methinks this
wise advice hath an ugly sound from lips
as young as yours. What mean you, Olaf?
speak."

The queen had spoken with majesty
and dignity but without hauteur, her soft
mellow tones breathing woman's sympathy,
though at the same time sounding the note
of woman's insatiable curiosity. Olaf
raised his head, and, opening wide his
great blue eyes, looked full at Grunhilde.
It was a strange look he gave her—a

dreamy, far-away, reminiscent look—but a look full of powerful concentration, of conscious power, a gaze at once sympathetic and controlling, introspective and search-ing, sorrowful and triumphant, loving yet challenging, a look that in these days would be termed mesmeric, and under its influence Grunhilde closed her eyes, while a scarcely perceptible shudder threw its tremors over her slender frame. I said it was a loving look, yet it was not a lover's look, but rather the reverential homage of a devoted subject than the passionate yearning of a sighing lover. All this took but a moment. There was a scarcely per-ceptible pause before Olaf replied to her question, but in this brief space of time each had seen something of the other's soul — *she* saw a man hardy, resolute, even fierce with man, yet tender as the dove with woman, daring all save that which might bring tears to bright eyes that should swim in joy ; *he* saw a woman tender, clinging in love, fierce in passion, uncompromising in ambition ; willing to dare all for love, yet more for power—

such were the sleeping souls hardly yet aroused which each saw in the other's breast.

The photographic view perturbed them, but Olaf, bowing, answered her : "Fair queen! Olaf's words have no meaning save that they bear unto thy mind. I deal not in riddles, O! Queen of Landsvag. I pray thee reproach me not for too great freedom. Thou hast said true, Olaf is young, yet, sweet queen, when thou didst busy thyself with chasing the bright-winged butterfly Olaf sat at the feet of the great Morgen, and from his lips learned the things he hath even now told to thee. Yea, queen, Olaf is young, but who in this kingdom beareth heavier loads?"

"Mistake me not, Olaf ; I do not chide; I but seek to know the news you bear our lord, the king—is it not the queen's duty to learn wherein she may aid her spouse and sovereign ?"

"Yea, queen ; but should she not hear that from her king and not from one of the lowliest of his subjects?" and Olaf again turned his eyes upon the maiden.

That look, full of compassion, of yearning love and fear, Grunhilde intercepted, and with a woman's intuition divining that the presence of this maiden was the cause of Olaf's silence, she turned to the women in waiting and said : " Leave us; we would be alone."

When the chamber was deserted she smiled sweetly on Olaf as she said : "You were right to hold your peace before the women, but now are you alone with your queen—speak."

Olaf shook his head. "Queen, I have no words for thee save the love and homage of thy most faithful servant."

Grunhilde began to grow impatient, she stamped her foot. "Have done with this unseemly trifling ! I saw the presence of the maiden, Hilda, whom you love, locked your too discreet tongue and so dismissed her.   Now are we alone ; speak ; I command you !   Where have you been ? "

" On the king's mission, queen."

" And that mission ? "

" To obey his orders."

" What report bring you back?"

"That I have fulfilled the mission entrusted to me."

"I have asked you what that mission was ; a queen does not repeat her question."

"And I have replied, queen."

The man stood stately, imperturbable, inscrutable ; the woman, with kindling eye and flushed cheek, watched him closely. Realizing that her queenship had no terrors for such a soul as his she tried another plan. Going up to him she laid her hand on his shoulder and softly said : "Olaf, is the friendship of Grunhilde the queen of less value to you than that of Grunhilde the maid? Do you no longer recall the days of our innocent childhood when we kept not so jealously our secrets?"

Olaf reached up, took the hand that rested on his shoulder, kissed it tenderly but reverently as might a brother, and answered :

"Grunhilde ! my more than sister, death shall claim me before I forget the days thou recallest, but we are chil-

dren no longer; fate separates us; thou art
now the queen, I the subject. Thou know-
est full well thou hast my allegiance, but
thou art unkind to press me; I hold my
honor above even thy sweet smile, and to
my king, and him alone, sweet Grunhilde,
will I render report of that I have done
and seen."

Grunhilde knit her brows.

"There be disturbing rumors abroad,
Olaf."

"Yea, queen; Olaf has heard them."

"Have you sought to find if there be
weight of truth in them? If so, the
queen should know, that she may aid her
liege lord in meeting the dangers which do
beset his path."

Olaf made no reply. The queen was
growing angry.

"Your queen spoke, Olaf," she said,
sharply.

"Olaf heard thee," was the quiet
reply.

"Then what saith Olaf?"

"Nothing, queen."

This was too much; she broke out:

"Rebellion beginneth early with you, seeing that you have this hour tendered your homage. Hath Olaf grown so mighty that he feareth not the anger of his queen ? Halfjord brooketh no insolence, and hath a long and heavy arm!" And the queen, with an indignant parting glance, swept from the room, leaving poor Olaf, firm in his resolution to speak only to the king, deeply distressed at the queen's evident displeasure, combined with the disquieting news he bore.

The young man was about to retire when a rustling sound caught his ear. As he looked up, a curtain at the other end of the chamber parted, and through the opening peered the half-frightened, half-expectant face of the girl, Hilda, and a very pretty picture she made, with her dark chestnut hair resting against the blue of the curtain, her bright face flushed with mingled expectation and trepidation. Seeing him alone, she advanced a step.

"Hilda," he said, in tones full of pathetic tenderness. "Olaf !"—she was in his arms.

Softly the young man smoothed away the curls that clustered about the girl's forehead, then taking her face between his hands, gazed earnestly and fondly at her, while she, with uplifted eyes, met his gaze with the trusting frankness of innocent love. " Olaf," she murmured, " My heart has been heavy in your absence."

Still caressing her soft and dimpled cheeks, the young man smiled complacently at her innocent confession of love, as he replied, "Olaf's heart knoweth neither peace nor rest save in Hilda's presence."

A glad smile flitted across her face but to be hidden beneath the heavy cloud of apprehension that rolled its dark pall again over her features. " Olaf, my heart is full of nameless terrors."

" What, little one ; what unkind dreams come in your virgin sleep ? Your days should be filled with peace and joy ; your nights with fair dreams of happy love ; what has Hilda to fear ? "

" Naught for Hilda ; much for Olaf. My heart misgives me when you go on

these long journeys, while even the gods
seem to have joined with ruthless men in
warring upon those who seek to hold the
thrones and homes of their fathers. When
you are away my heart tells me of your
dangers; for at such times a strange and
stifling flutter stops my eager breath, and
on my heart is burned as with an iron the
words, 'Olaf is in danger!'"

"Peace, child! Olaf loveth too well your
sweet love to say you do love Olaf too
well; nay, love Olaf even more, maiden;
let your heart never forget him; but in
loving Olaf seek not to make your love
the father of that foul bastard Fear. In that
time the king shall name the fair Hilda
shall be Olaf's bride; but Hilda will also
be mother of Olaf's unborn sons; then see
to it, timid maiden, that your present fears
be not so deeply graven on your tender
heart as to make of those sons whom you
shall bear but cringing, craven cowards."

"Olaf, upbraid me not, I pray you; my
heart is torn with anxious fears, yet those
fears are but for you. Hilda is no coward
save when love bids her fear. Hilda hath

heart to bear a son as valiant as any in Landsvag."

"Sweet one, I did not chide; I but sought to stifle your needless fears. But come, Hilda, tell me what you know of these happenings that bring disquietude to your loving heart."

"Olaf, the queen saith Harold, he whom they call 'The Fair-haired,' hangeth even upon the borders of our land, of which his covetous heart would despoil us. Tell me, Olaf, is this so?"

Olaf knit his brows in a dark frown as he answered rather sharply: "What hath a young maiden with such tales? These things are for men. Grunhilde is a good queen, but overfond of stirring with her slender hand the pot in which are brewed the histories of peoples. Listen not to her, Hilda, else will you too grow ambitious, and in feeding ambition's poisonous weed forget to water the fragrant flower of love."

She shook her head sadly. "Olaf, you know me not if you do think I have stomach for such things. I but hear with my ears, see with my eyes for the sake of him whom I love. If Harold comes, then will Olaf go forth to attack him, and I fear me I shall die at thought of your too great chance of death."

"Olaf has done battle before and doubtless will again, but let not that thought disturb the sweet joy of our meeting."

"Ah ! Olaf, that you do not tell me what I have heard is but idle tales disturbs me the more. But that is not the whole I would tell."

Olaf's interest increased. "What more, Hilda ?" he asked, briskly.

"It is even said that Olaf, Halfjord's trusted vassal, hath been into Harold's very camp seeking if he might not turn aside the sword from this land. This is the reason given why Olaf hath not been seen at the festive board nor in the chase his heart loveth ; say they true, Olaf ?"

"Hilda," he answered sternly, "Within the hour, in your very presence, I did refuse to disclose aught to our good queen, thereby much vexing her ; you do wrong to question me."

"Nay, I seek not those secrets you say are so heavy ; I did but think if that they say be true Olaf should have told Hilda of the great danger which should beset him, and not have left without even see-ing Hilda."

"Girl ! where I have been matters not ; yet this will I say : I dared not see you for fear sight of your sweet face, your tear-washed eyes, would move my heart to too great tenderness for those things I must do."

These were grateful words ; she smiled sweetly at him, but continued : "Even more disturbs Hilda's heart."

"Your fears are many as the sands of the seashore. What more?"

"The queen is angered, Olaf."

"Yea, she seeks to rule : Halfjord she may rule, but Olaf only through his king. I love our queen, as you well know, but women have no place in those movements which may make or wreck kingdoms. She is vexed, but tomorrow will have forgot it and be the Grunhilde of old to her playmate Olaf."

"I fear not so," was the doubting reply.

" Why?"

The girl did not answer for a moment ; she stood seemingly lost in thought, but finally lifting her head, looked him full in the face as she asked hesitatingly: "Olaf, often have you told me of the days of your childhood when Grunhilde was your playmate—your sister ; have you never thought the love that, in the child, was a sister's, in the woman might be more ?"

Olaf's great eyes opened in unfeigned astonishment.   A smile of incredulity, amusement, was wreathing about his lips, when, without giving him time to reply, she added in a tone of mournful conviction, "I have."

Olaf's first impulse was to burst out laughing, but, noting her serious, pained expression, he checked himself and waited for her to continue.   She spoke with difficulty, as though the words hurt her: "Olaf is valiant and noble ; Grunhilde hath eyes, a heart as well ; Olaf's heart returneth not the tenderness of Grunhilde's ; Olaf heed-eth not her words. The queen is angry, yet is the queen not so angry as the woman ; the queen may forgive, the woman, never."

" Hilda, your young fancy findeth in me so much to love you may not see how other women should not love Olaf. You are silly, child, yet is it a silliness that delights my heart. But harbor not in your mind such thoughts as these. It were death to you, to me as well, were those words spoken to another save me."

"That know I, Olaf, and I tremble as with an ague at very thought of such thoughts, yet does my woman's heart tell me I am right."

Provoked at her persistence, Olaf, to whom it all seemed the silly fear of a timid woman, chided her sharply. The tears came into her eyes, but she made no reply, and after a few moments he said : "Come, little one, this is but a sorry meeting after my absence. Dry your bright eyes and drive away these troublous thoughts. I have done great service for our king, and this night shall I ask of him your hand as my reward. ˆNor do I fear he will refuse me."

" Halfjord might grant your prayer, but Grunhilde, never ; and if Grunhilde refuses then does Halfjord deny."

"This again? Hilda, you grow foolish."

"Nay; hear me out, Olaf. During your absence Alric has hotly pressed his suit."

"What ! that spawn of a demon ! Alric of the bloody hair dare to raise his eyes to look upon Hilda ! Have a care for yourself, Alric !" And the young man, grinding his teeth with rage, shook his clenched fist in the air in mute defiance, and began striding with feverish haste up and down the long room, while Hilda, scarcely able to keep up with him, continued :

"Yes, Olaf, Alric of the bloody hair seeks Hilda for his bride. You need not me to tell you that he finds no favor in my eyes ; but, Olaf, he hath won a powerfully ally."

" In whom?"

" In the queen."

" The queen !" Olaf stopped short in

his amazement, and turned almost sav-
agely on the girl.

"Yes, the queen, Olaf; shall I tell you
all?"

"Yes," he muttered between his clenched
teeth.

"Alric won the queen's ear and she
spoke to me urging me to listen kindly to
his suit. I told her I could not love him,
and she said that mattered not. She per-
sisted; I pleaded; she grew vexed, and
finally I told her I was betrothed to an-
other; she demanded his name; I gave it,
and she flew into a terrible rage, upbraided
me, and ended by saying I should take the
husband my sovereign chose for me. Olaf,
the queen is against us."

"And the king?" he asked.

"Will do aught to please his queen;
remember, she is yet a bride."

"True; are you not dreaming, Hilda?
Can it be as you say?"

"Olaf, would Hilda hug so dreadful a
dream to her breast, or find room in her
heart, which beats but for you, for sense-
less fears so harrowing to the soul?"

Olaf walked in gloomy silence to the open casement, and, stretching out his hand toward the rolling valley far beneath, said in half-soliloquy : " This, then, is the reward for faithful service. To Morgen, my father, this land owes its power; to me does Halfjord owe his throne; Grunhilde her king. For Landsvag's sake have I dared do that which would blanch the cheek of swaggering knights who elbow one another before the throne I helped to make. A stripling I, and yet for Halfjord I do bear upon these young shoulders a weight beneath which a giant might totter. While Halfjord seeks the luring pleasures of life's morn I do support the throne whereon he gaily disports himself, and that he may taste the rich wine of lusty youth do grovel out my halcyon days in the noisome cellar of politics beneath the foot of the throne. A thankless task at best, yet have I never murmured nor yet have sought a boon, holding myself above the fawning sycophants who do lick the hand that feeds them and then cry, ' More ! more ! ' Shall Olaf now approach

on bended knee that throne he made and
ask of him, the king whom Olaf seated
upon that throne, as sole reward for faith-
ful service done, the hand of this most
gentle maid, but to be spurned like a dog;
nay, more, to see this lovely casket of
a lovelier soul thrown as a sop unto a
snarling hound, sired by a demon out of a
she-wolf ? Landsvag, I love your valleys,
each separate ragged peak of yours doth
rest its base upon my heart, yet will I not
brook this even for your sake. Oh ! Mor-
gen ! let your departed shade guide me in
this hour ! See ! here comes Halfjord,
returning from the chase ; a goodly sight
those valiant men do make ; cheek by jowl
they ride, yet can Olaf pit them one
against the other and overturn them even
as they have stricken down the boar their
menials bear behind them. Look to thy-
self, Halfjord ! This night shall Olaf
demand of thee the price of his service—
beware if thou refuse him ! "

Hilda had stood in breathless suspense
during this outburst ; not daring to speak,
she yet feared to keep silence, but now

approaching steps were heard, and, run-
ning to the window, she plucked Olaf's
sleeve.   He turned

"Go! some one cometh," she whispered.
The man hesitated for a moment, then,
grasping her hand, said : "Tonight!"
and went hurriedly out just as two of the
queen's ladies appeared at the other end
of the apartment.

CHAPTER II

It is necessary to take the reader back for a brief sketch of the events leading up to the opening of the previous chapter.

Norway was cut up into petty principalities or kingdoms, while each separate kingdom had usually its rival claimants for the throne, nor was Landsvag any exception to the rule.

After years of struggle and bloodshed Morgen, Olaf's father, had succeeded in firmly establishing Heljar upon the throne of Landsvag, but old Morgen died, and the contending factions, seeing in his death their opportunity, renewed their efforts to overturn the throne.

Heljar was not strong enough to crush them, and his power was crumbling away when Olaf, then a mere lad, took up arms for the perpetuation of that which his father had established. His successes soon made him popular. Recruits daily

flocked to his banner. Old men hearkened
readily to the wise counsels of this re-
markáble youth. The conspirators, find-
ing their cause lost, hastened to make
peace on any terms, but Heljar died just
at the time when Olaf's masterful leader-
ship had assured him a tranquil reign.
The young man now found the crown of
Landsvag within his reach. Had he seized
it his sovereignty would have been recog-
nized with rejoicing such was the hold he
had gained upon the people's hearts. But,
wonderfully true to principle for a man of
his time, he scorned the tempting bait and
caused Heljar's son, Halfjord, to be pro-
claimed.

Discontent broke out afresh. Thous-
ands who would have bent the knee to
the redoubtable Olaf were less ready to re-
cognize the untried Halfjord. But Olaf
crushed the rebellion with an iron hand,
and, seating the son as firmly on the throne
as his father had the father, he stood im-
perturbable, immovable, invincible, a liv-
ing rampart between his king and his
country's destroyers ; nor were there any

in Landsvag who dared face his menacing frown or meet the force of his uplifted arm. While Olaf stood on guard Landsvag was safe from the vipers warmed in her own bosom.

The king and his sturdy supporter were of relatively the same age, had grown up together and even borne arms together in support of the cause so dear to both, yet were they utterly dissimilar, seemingly having nothing in common save the rule of Heljar's house. Halfjord was generous, sympathetic, open in speech as in heart, free of confidence, quick in resentment, yet ready to forgive. Olaf, equally brave, reckless, a veritable god of war, yet off the field calm, inscrutable ; inviting confidences, never imparting them ; watchful, suspicious, guarded, of few words and those to the point ; not without generosity nor devoid of sympathy, with a kindly heart, a wealth of natural affection, but presenting so cold an exterior as to have it said he knew no feeling. Halfjord, in a burst of generous sentiment, would forgive and load with honors his

most implacable foe should he present his
hypocritical face in humble supplication ;
Olaf, like a Brutus, would slay his own son
rather than endanger the peace and safety
of the state to which he owed his fealty.
The king, slothful and indolent in work,
eager, impetuous in pursuit of pleasure,
ever susceptible to bright eyes, from his
earliest youth involved in entangling al-
liances with the fair dames who graced his
father's court ; the minister, indefatigable,
untiring in work, cold and undemonstra-
tive amid scenes of pleasure save for a flash
from his eye, the heightened color of his
cheek when his own hand slew the boar,
seemingly unconscious of female charms
until the fair Hilda crossed his path.

Such were these two men within whose
breasts were locked the destinies of Lands-
vag.

Halfjord had been king something over
two years at the time our story opens. His
throne steadied by the hand of Olaf, he
(the king) had found time to look around
him. His generous, impulsive nature had
won him friends even among his former

bitter foes, and now the court was thronged
with those who but a brief space of time
before had sought his ruin, death, or both.
Foremost among his erstwhile antago-
nists was Alric (called "The Bloody Hair,"
from the intense, peculiar red of his locks),
who now seemed to enjoy the full confi-
dence of the king and was fast worming
himself into favor with the bride-queen.

Olaf, doubting Alric's sincerity, had on
more than one occasion warned Halfjord
against him, but the latter replied by good-
naturedly chiding him for his unkind sus-
picions and continued in the even tenor of
his way, so that Olaf ceased speaking but
did not stop watching.

Surrounded by friends who vied with
one another in courting his favor, his days
full of sunshine, his throne rooted, Half-
jord had looked about him for a queen to
share with him that throne, and his choice
fell upon Grunhilde—a typical northern
beauty, with rich golden hair, deep-blue
eyes full of passionate tenderness, a match-
less form. She had long been the pride of
Landsvag, and many a luckless swain had

sighed out his heart at her feet only to bewail her iciness. A famous beauty, yet of irreproachable character, of noble, even semi-royal blood, and adored by the people of Landsvag, she was a most fitting consort for the young king, and the entire kingdom gave itself up to rejoicing for three days when it became known that Halfjord and Grunhilde were betrothed.

Grunhilde was the daughter of a cousin of King Heljar; her father had fallen battling with Morgen for their king, and left her, an orphan child, a ward to Morgen, who had carefully nourished her, bestowing on her the affection of a father.

Thus it was that Grunhilde and Olaf had grown from childhood to womanhood and manhood in all the close intimacy of brother and sister, while unconsciously to themselves the absence of such relationship added a peculiar charm to this same intimacy—a charm which might have been dangerous had not Olaf so early in life taken up the work his father had laid down. Indeed, there were not lacking those who said the mischief had been already done, and that had Olaf but spoken Grunhilde would have been his wife rather than Queen of Landsvag. But Olaf did not speak and she became Halfjord's bride, Landsvag's queen, else might this story never have been told.

How strange that a few words hastily spoken, or not spoken at all—words to many but an unintelligible combination of letters or of sounds — may dam the sweeping current of history, make kingdoms and overturn dynasties. Truly in this world there is nothing small nor insignificant ; even as all values are relative so is the importance of all things. The gnat may, under given circumstances, be the agent of destruction as great as the mighty elephant. A rose, a word, a tear—the rose withers, the word is forgot, the tear dries, yet the soft and dainty bloom of the rose was the guerdon of mighty battalions in a ruthless war. Why ? Because in angry discussion one plucked a red rose, one a white. The faltering "Yes" of a timid woman, rather breathed than spoken, less than half a century later trampled

beneath iron hoofs the torn and throbbing
heart of humanity, made a funeral pyre of
the wrecked remains of empires, until, in
a sea of blood, went down the strangest
star that ever has flashed upon the eastern
sky. The half-concealed tears of a mother
raised aloft that torch of liberty lit upon
Concord's plain ; that torch, before whose
blinding blaze in sweeping circles search-
ing out the dark and hidden corners of
the earth, the sun of heaven hid his duller
face. A word spoken or unspoken, a rose
plucked or unplucked, a tear shed or un-
shed—no, there is nothing small in this
world we call our own. Handle the wren
as you would the eagle, the worm as the
deadly cobra ; beware of the teeth of the
mouse as you would of those of the frenzied
lion, and, when tempted to think slight-
ingly of the insignificance of aught which
comes to you, remember that in the end
but six feet of this vast earth is yours, and
even that but by suffrance—six feet ; a
bagatelle, but a handful of earth, and still
enough to cover all that is mortal of you,
proud man ! that findeth littleness in this

world, but seeth not your own dwarfish-
ness.

If the gossips of Landsvag were right
Grunhilde was queen because Olaf had
not asked her to share his fate ; but
whether it be that the unspoken word was
the cause or that she gave her heart with
her hand to Halfjord, the facts are that
some three weeks or more before this story
opens Grunhilde and Halfjord were wed-
ded with great pomp amid the rejoicings
of all their subjects.

But this is again anticipating, and once
more must the reader, with kind patience,
return with us to the time before the
nuptials.

Though Halfjord might, thanks to Olaf,
feel safe from enemies within his kingdom,
yet was not Landsvag safe from foes with-
out. Many of the petty princes around
her looked with longing eyes upon her
rich and smiling valleys, and, had they
felt strong enough, would have overrun
her, but not able, unaided, to overcome
her, and too jealous of one another to com-
bine, they now contented themselves with

armed incursions, forays across the bor-
der, harassing the people and retiring
laden with spoils before troops arrived.

These expeditions were met with counter
invasions, undertaken for the purpose of
teaching these people a lesson, and the
hand of Olaf, who was on the frontier
whenever he could be spared from the
court, fell heavy on these marauding
neighbors.

Life next door to a thief who seeks every
opportunity of despoiling you has few
charms. The people of the border ap-
pealed to Halfjord, to Olaf, nor did
they cry in vain. Each freebooting ex-
pedition met a well-merited retribution,
but the most guilty always escaped—the
inoffensive peasant gave up his worthless (?)
life while his thievish lord lived for another
pilfering raid. Wearied by these persist-
ent attacks, indignant at the loss of life
and property suffered by Landsvag's serfs
and small landowners, Olaf had for a
year prayed Halfjord's consent to a great
expedition, organized for the purpose of
subjugating these disturbing neighbors.

His idea was, since they would not other-
wise be taught, they should be forced into
submission to Halfjord and their domains
blotted out from their now independent
position on Norway's political map, and be
made dependencies of Landsvag.   It was
to be a war of subjugation, of extermina-
tion if necessary.

"I will trample these robbers beneath
my horses' hoofs, crush these parasites in
the hollow of my hand," he said to Half-
jord.   But the latter was loth to undertake
so great a task; hesitated, temporized, and
would doubtless have finally refused had
not a particularly daring and successful
raid into the very heart of his kingdom
roused his kingly ire.   In a fit of impetuous
rage at the bold audacity of these knaves
he gave the desired consent.

Olaf lost no time in preparing for this
expedition, which he now fondly dreamed
should make Landsvag foremost among
the powers of the North.   But Halfjord
interposed ;   his wedding was set within a
few months ;   he could not have all his
valiant men in the field at such a time ;

the expedition must be postponed until
after that ceremony, when he would make
no further objection ; though, forsooth,
after his first violent outburst of temper
he regretted having sanctioned the enter-
prise and gave but poor support to his
minister. Indeed, he would probably have
entirely withdrawn his consent were it not
for the fact that while he loved he also
feared Olaf, and dared not disavow openly
that to which he had given his approval,
lest Olaf, in anger, should leave him to his
own resources, which were few.

In vain did Olaf entreat, even advising
that the postponement be of the wedding
rather than of the expedition.   In vain
did he warn the king that the second sum-
mons to arms would be less eagerly obeyed
than the first.   Halfjord was obdurate ;
Grunhilde first ; peace and protection,
glory and greatness after.   Concealing his
chagrin as well as he was able, Olaf sus-
pended preparations and impatiently waited
the day when, riding at the head of Lands-
vag's troops, the incarnation of war, he
might vindicate before the world the prow-

ess of his native land. During the not
entirely amicable interviews between the
two at this time Halfjord frequently re-
ferred to the now unusual quietude of the
borders, arguing from that a lack of neces-
sity for the drastic measures proposed by
Olaf, and, indeed, an ominous peace
reigned at present over this distracted
portion of the land—a peace as sudden
as the frightened stillness of the air before
the approaching storm.

"We have taught them even now,
Olaf," he said. "A wise master flogs not
too often his menials."

"True ; nor doth a wise king give into
the hands of others a rod with which to
beat his own subjects."

"What mean you ? "

" Thou knowest my meaning, Halfjord."

"Nay ; make it plain unto me."

"This is my meaning, king : If these
too arrogant thieves be not rudely handled
then do they call the peace we give them
our weakness. The rod thou hast put into
their hands is this thy present delay."

" Why call you our peaceful disposition

a rod with which to beat our faithful servants ? Your wit hath greater depth than we can fathom ; we would be at peace with the world during our coming nuptials."

" Yea, king ; I would we were ever at peace ; but these our warlike intentions have been noised abroad. The report of them hath reached the ears of those we would disarm, and the false peace thou pridest thyself upon is but as the sleep of the silent waves before the whistling wind hath lashed them into fell and frightful fury. Dost think they rest ? Nay ! with a robber's ready wit for a space of time they hide, but in their hiding-place do hatch foul schemes against the land we would protect. While we, in idle dalliance, do wait to dance attendance upon the fair consort thou hast chosen, they gather together their tried and trusty followers, and, when we take the field, Olaf will find for every man he thought to meet an hundred lances. Ah ! king ; with the too soft pleasantries of idle youth thou dost imperil thy throne ! "

"Olaf, you have too stern a mind for youth; you find no pleasure in those sweet drops of honeyed life that fall into the hungry mouths of the young ; go, cast away your gloomy thoughts until your king is wed, then mount your steed and seek the bloody fray for which your nerves are tingling, and Halfjord will not say you nay. But this I tell you, Olaf—for once your mind hath lost its cunning ; these troublesome marauders are quiet through fear of our punishment—through dread of your long arm, and not with foolish intent to combine in opposition to Landsvag's valiant men."

"Nay, king ; but hear me, I pray thee —"

"No more today, Olaf ; you are wrong, I say."

Olaf went out, disgusted, disheartened; and the news of the day showed that Half-jord was wrong while Olaf was not right.

When he left the king's presence Olaf was informed that Jorg, baron of one of Landsvag's border dependencies, craved audience with him, and, going to a small closet where, when with the king, he received the emissaries of state, he summoned the visitor to attend him.

While waiting, Olaf paced in feverish restlessness the narrow confines of his closet. He was not entirely free from that trait of human nature which rejoices in the fulfillment of its own prophecy at whatever cost. The sweetest words (to the man himself) that man ever utters are, "I told you so!" And even though the faithful fulfillment of that he has foretold presages death and ruin, yet the would-be self-believed prophet walks triumphantly through this wreck of human happiness, and before each ghastly corpse complacently murmurs, "I told you so!"

As Olaf strode up and down waiting the appearance of his man he muttered to himself from time to time, giving voice to his troublous thoughts: "This Jorg bringeth news of that I warned the king against. Even now the hostile legions gather against our land, and Jorg cometh to tell us that the banner of Landsvag hath once more been dragged in the slime of the earth. The foolish dalliance of this our king hath reddened our soil with blood of many faithful servants." He clenched his hand and, stamping his foot, exclaimed, "If I were king—" At this moment Jorg was ushered into his presence.

The baron bowed respectfully and waited for Olaf to address him, as though he had been in the presence of the king himself, and Olaf, critically surveying him from head to foot, asked : "Whence come you, Jorg, spurring so hotly ?"

"From my estates, Olaf," was the reply.

"You come early unto the king's wedding."

"I come not to the nuptials of the king."

"Nay? Wherefore, then, ride you so hastily, Jorg ?"

"To gain your ear, Olaf."

"My ear ? That have you even now; naught may Jorg ask that Olaf will not grant if it be the king's good pleasure."

"I ask nothing."

"None seek the ear of a minister save those who have prayers to offer."

"Nay, Olaf, there are you wrong. Those who have much to *say* seek the king's minister even as those who would *ask* much."

"And you, Jorg?"

"Have much to tell."

"Then speak. The border barons have again let loose their minions on your lands?"

"No, Olaf."

"They plan expeditions against you and us?"

"No, Olaf, the border troubles me no more."

"Then what brings you hither?" asked Olaf, somewhat testily.

Jorg approached closer, and taking the young man by the sleeve, said: "Olaf is brave, but Olaf needeth an arm of iron, a heart of stone, for that which cometh!"

"What mean you, man? You deal in unseemly riddles."

"Olaf, the border hath been quiet as the sleeping lamb for these two moons."

"Yea, that know I."

"But know you the cause?"

"They plan against Landsvag?"

"Not so, Olaf; they seek to save themselves."

"From whom?"

The baron dropped his voice to a whisper as he replied: "From Harold, the Fair-haired."

Olaf started.

Often had he heard that name; the name of the scourge of southern Norway, but he had never dreamt of the sword of Harold piercing the very vitals of the country to its extremity—his own loved Landsvag.

"Have they then sold themselves unto Harold, and go they south to fight with him? If this be so then is our task easier and we shall present the fair Grunhilde a coronet of circling baronies embraced within Landsvag's extended arms," he said, after a pause.

"Nay, Olaf," replied Jorg, sadly, "they go south, but they go to withstand the mighty army Harold bringeth; if now Landsvag join them then would we crush this haughty Harold and make of these men faithful allies in place of careless robbers."

For a moment Olaf regarded with unfeigned admiration this man who, having spent his checkered life on the border, where few opportunities for the study of statecraft presented themselves, had yet so bluntly spoken the thoughts of his own mind, that mind schooled in diplomacy as the arm was in the heavy blows of the fray, but he sought to draw the man out. "And if we join not with them, Jorg?" he asked.

"Then will Harold surely overcome them and on the borders of Landsvag will be not many small provinces, each jealous of the other and too weak to fight us, but the compact kingdom of this wizard of the South who seemeth to do all things. When that day cometh then will Harold take from us even Landsvag."

"The words of Jorg have an unpleasant sound in mine ears."

"Yea, and a bitter taste have they in Jorg's mouth, but that they are true none know so well as him to whom I speak."

"Nay, Jorg, let not your words run so fast; Olaf keepeth his own counsel."

"That know I; nor do I expect that Olaf will aught reveal unto me, but Olaf's thoughts are even as I say."

"You are a shrewd fellow, Jorg. Now what would you that we do?"

"What? Why, Jorg would have you do that which even now you have in mind."

"And that, Jorg?"

"Olaf, my hair is white; your pleasantries please me not; but, though you do seek to make sport of Jorg, yet for love of that land I call mine own will I tell you that naught remains to Landsvag save to make peace at any price with these our former enemies and in concert with them present a solid wall to these invaders—a wall built of human hearts, beating in lusty bodies; a wall that shall mark the border line between liberty and oppression; a wall that shall teach Harold and the world that Landsvag holds its liberty inviolate."

Jorg paused for breath; Olaf, advancing, took him by the hand and said: "Jorg, you have even spoken Olaf's mind."

Jorg unhesitatingly grasped the out-
stretched hand.

"And is Olaf now with Jorg?" he asked.

The young man, still holding the sinewy
hand, replied: "Olaf is ever for Lands-
vag."

"Yea, but Jorg's plan saves Landsvag."

"That doth it, wherefore is Olaf for
Jorg's plan."

The old man brightened up at this dec-
laration. "Now, will Landsvag eat out the
heart of this wild boar of the South!" he
exclaimed, enthusiastically.

Olaf made no reply to this outburst save
to dismiss Jorg, bidding him hold himself
in readiness to wait upon him when sum-
moned.

Left alone, the young minister sat for
some time wrapped in deep and gloomy
thought. Once he exclaimed aloud: "If
he refuse!" But at the very thought he knit
his brows into a heavy frown, while fire
flashed from his eyes and the lines of his
mouth went down into fixed and stern re-
solve. Presently he arose and, still with
thoughtful mien, went in search of the king

He went first to Halfjord's own apart-
ments, entering, with the familiarity of a
trusted friend; next to the audience cham-
ber, but the king was not to be found in
either place.   Questioning one of the
young gentlemen in the king's ante-room
he received no information save that he
must be in the castle since they were not
advised of his going out.   Hardly waiting
for answers to his questions he moved im-
patiently about the vast pile seeking every-
where for his master, but not finding him
until, just as he was about to give up the
search and, returning to the king's apart-
ments, await him there, one of his own
servants meeting him told him where the
king might be found.

CHAPTER III

Olaf found his majesty closeted in a small chamber in a remote part of the building, where, with a few boon companions, he was indulging in those wild revels so pleasing to his vagrant fancies. There was a scarcely perceptible sneer on the young man's face as, entering unannounced, he surveyed the scene, and looked with cold disdain upon the flushed faces and bloodshot eyes of the half-startled sycophants as he walked steadily across the room to where the king was seated.

Half ashamed at being caught in such a condition, half fearful of interruption, wholly conscious of inferiority, Halfjord no sooner saw Olaf than he rudely accosted him with, "Why hath Olaf's gloomy face and frowning brow disturbed us in our merriment?"

Disgusted with the scene before him,

angered at the king's reception, Olaf yet
gave no outward sign of his thoughts, but,
bowing respectfully, said: "Olaf hath
sought thee, king, for urgent reasons; I
crave an audience with thee, Halfjord."

But the king was in no humor for busi-
ness. "Yea," he said, "I even thought
you came to break upon these, our pleas-
antries, with some of your dull stories of
statecraft, but not tonight, sage Olaf, not
tonight; it were enough to spend these
pretty days with ear attuned to doleful
sounds of work, the which you chant in
solemn strains from morn till eve. A day
with you hath earned me needed rest — I
will not work this night."

"King," repeated Olaf, "I crave a word
with thee."

"What? Hath the man no wit? The
king said he will not work this night,"
called out Alric, insolently.

Though Olaf with the king was long-suf-
fering, he was quick enough to resent any
affront, real or fancied, that might be
offered by any below the throne. Turning

to face Alric, who sat near where he stood, he spoke with meaning emphasis: "Olaf hath wit to know a one-time traitor who now doth lick in fulsome fawning the hand of that king he would have slain, and, knowing him, Alric, Olaf hath wit neither to trust nor to love him."

The shot struck home. Alric flushed, grew pale, stirred uneasily in his seat, finally ending an awkward pause by asking threateningly, "Olaf speaks of whom?"

Olaf fixed on his antagonist a searching, challenging glance as he replied in low, steady tones, "Of Alric I speak!"

The man sprang to his feet and, drawing his sword, rushed at Olaf, who had already put himself on guard awaiting the attack. The room was in an uproar; men rushed between the angry combatants crying out: "Sheath your swords!" "What! In the king's presence?"

Halfjord himself called out: "Gentlemen, ye seek took too serious sport: put up those stinging toys; he who draweth blood shall feel my anger." At sound of the king's voice Olaf lowered his blade and, again turning, faced Halfjord. Bowing respectfully, he said : " Thy pardon, king."

" We like not your diversions, Olaf," replied the king, angrily. " You are too hot for the sword, too cold for those pleasures that do lend flavor unto life. Wherefore are you and Alric enemies ? "

" King, Olaf hath no enemies save they be thine," was the reply.

Alric sprang up shouting : " King, give me leave, I pray thee ! I may not coldly brook his words."

" Peace, Alric ; now are you too hot."

" He hath called me thy enemy," was the sullen reply, as Alric resumed his seat.

" I will no more of this quarrel, which hath so marred our pleasure," said Halfjord. " Drink, gentlemen, drink to the fair Grunhilde—a cup for Olaf,"—to one of the menials near him—" Drink to our queen, Olaf."

The toast was quaffed with boisterous enthusiasm. Olaf drank in silence and, when he could be heard, said : " To fair Grunhilde have I drank with loyal heart,

O king, but now, even in the face of thy
displeasure, do I repeat my prayer for thine
ear this night; yea, king, this I ask even
for Grunhilde's sake." The king stared at
him in amazement. "What mean you,
Olaf? Hath aught befell our betrothed
queen ?"

"Nay, king, Grunhilde is well."

"Then doth Halfjord see not the point
of that you say."

Olaf stepped to the king's side and
whispered, "King, I have that to tell which
doth affect the throne whereon thou shalt
seat the fair Grunhilde, hence say I for her
sake hear me. It behooves us to act at
once, wherefore I pray thee to hear me
this night. King, for thy throne's sake
hear me !" But Halfjord broke out into a
loud, half-drunken laugh, and, pounding
the table with his great fist, fairly yelled,
"He talketh but of affairs of state as
though the day had not hours enough
for such dry food to our youthful minds.
Ha ! ha !"

"Ha ! ha !" echoed the parasites around
him. "Nay, good Olaf, too close attention

to this your heavy task I fear me will drive you mad. As though the state might not live through the night, while we in sweet merriment disport ourselves. If the pillars of our state be crumbling have we not swords to hold them up ? "

"Yea ! yea ! " shouted the revellers, rising in their seats and brandishing aloft their blades, with fierce oaths and lusty cheers.

Waving his hand for silence Halfjord continued, "Leave these dull and heavy cares for the morrow, Olaf, and this night join us in our gay diversions. A place at the board for Olaf ! "

But the young man, seemingly heedless of the invitation, stood like a rock for a moment, then, seeing the futility of further effort, turned and moved slowly to the door. Just before passing the threshold he again faced the boisterous crowd, and, in solemn tones that thrilled the hearts of his listeners, said, "King, hear Olaf, and when thy power hath passed, remember his words : Though thou dost revel by night, there be those who use the night for

making of the day that cometh after.
Oh! Halfjord, my king, my friend, be-
ware of him who sleepeth not nor revelleth
by night !"

"What mean you?" cried the now
startled king, but Olaf had disappeared,
leaving on the fevered brains of the care-
less bacchanalians the effect of a grue-
some spectre. Some there were who rallied
shortly from the sudden fear that had
seized them, while others, knowing Olaf's
keen insight, felt that the warning uttered
by the departing minister was not an
empty flourish, and foremost among these
latter was the king, who took but little
pleasure in the gay badinage that once
more ricocheted around the board.   Alric,
who had drank deeply before the interrup-
tion, was now even more devoted to the
cup, and in an excess of wine-heated valor
cried out, "Ah ! king, if thou hadst not
prevented I should have cut his gloomy
heart out of his sour-faced body !"

"Nay, Alric," the king spoke musingly,
"Olaf is too good a minister, you, too
good a friend, to be at each other's throats;

Landsvag hath need of you both." Shortly
after this the king rose and the revellers,
with unsteady steps, sought their couches.

In the meantime Olaf, on his way from
this scene, had encountered Jorg, who,
knowing that the minister would lose no
time in acquainting Halfjord with the situ-
ation, asked the result of his interview.
Olaf replied that the king could not see
him until morning, but the old man knew
Halfjord's weakness as well as he did
Olaf's strength, and divining the reason of
the delay, said bitterly, "So the King of
Landsvag prefereth dining with courtesans,
bastards and drunkards to looking after
the crown his father left him.   Then may
he lose it when he least expects ; truly he
who upholds the crown should wear it.
The throne holdeth not always the proper
man."   Olaf sharply rebuked him for the
implied treason of his speech, and they
separated just as the king's companions
came reeling in drunken mirth from the
scene of their orgies.

On the morrow Olaf sought the king
early, finding him ready this time to hear

what he would say, seeking indeed with a sovereign's graciousness to rub out the ugly marks of a king's displeasure, but even at his best Halfjord seemed to find it a heavy task to take life seriously, and no sooner had Olaf told him of Jorg's self-appointed mission than he smilingly said, "Hath old Jorg's excited dream disturbed the rest of the lusty Olaf? Methinks mine eyes might never know the sweet caress of sleep did I believe my throne as shaky as you would make appear, good Olaf."

"King, these are no idle dreams; thou hast heard of Harold, the Fair-haired, the scourge of southern Norway, who seeks to grasp within his mailed hand this continent?"

"Yea, Olaf, but not even this Harold may break the solid ranks of Landsvag when Olaf is at their head, wherefore I disturb me not. If he comes we fight; if we fight, then do we vanquish him; is not that enough?"

"Nay, king, Landsvag has not strength alone to crush Harold; we do need allies."

" I like not too well the allies of war ; they find it an easy task to be enemies in peace. Where would Olaf seek these allies ? "

"Among the barons on our border, king."

" What l Would Olaf sue for peace to men against whom he even now would be leading Landsvag's troops were it not for our kingly protest ? "

" Yea, king, Olaf would do aught for sake of this loved land."

"And have you no greater wit than to trust these old-time enemies who would join our banner but to betray us ? "

" Nay, king, even now they gather to protect themselves ; if they should unite with us, then in betraying us would they also sell their own possessions."

"Olaf, you have a searching mind and study these things when Halfjord seeks amusement, and yet methinks in this your wit hath fault, for these whom you would gather under our colors are but as robbers —they know no fealty save to their own interest, and I think the king who rested

on promise of their support would find
that same oath but a rotten prop.   Half-
jord will trust Landsvag to Olaf."

These last words were spoken kindly,
affectionately, as to a tried and trusted
friend; Olaf acknowledged the compli-
ment with a bow while he replied with
much show of feeling : "Halfjord, Olaf
thanketh thee for these thy kind words,
which are passing sweet unto mine ears,
but Olaf is one man and no more; I will
do all, dare all, for the sake of this fair
land, and Olaf hath, too, a stout arm that
breaketh where it striketh; but I beseech
thee, Halfjord, no more king than friend,
no less friend than king, turn not a deaf
ear to these solemn words.   Oh! Half-
jord, bethink thee; wouldst thou give unto
the lovely Grunhilde a crown that knoweth
no life save in name ?   Landsvag is val-
iant, but Landsvag may not unaided with-
stand the hosts of Harold; if thou dost sit
in indolent indecision Harold will over-
come these border barons and then, with
none to dispute his way, will march upon
us, bringing with him the loathsome chain

of servile dependence; but if Landsvag, in league with her neighbors, shall meet the arrogant Harold, then shall we tear his great army into bleeding fragments and, that done, may turn our eyes upon these too lawless pilferers. Halfjord, Landsvag alone cannot prevail, but with those who now present their iron faces to this resistless demon's march enrolled under our banner, then may we toss dirt in the faces of Harold's vaunting legions and laugh at their impotent rage. Halfjord, thou art king, I pray thee now be a true king, seeking but the good of this thy favored land!"

The king made no reply and, after a brief pause, Olaf continued: "King, Jorg waits thy bidding; even now is his horse saddled that he may swiftly bear thy message unto those who, once enemies, are now much needed friends."

But Halfjord was as obstinate as he was lazy; indeed, his obstinacy was doubtless but the result of an indolence that refused to press to its best efforts a mind naturally gifted.

"No, Olaf," he finally said, "no treaty with these spoilers of our land."

The young minister, aghast, seemed unable to comprehend the full meaning of his king's words.

"What!" he gasped, "Doth Landsvag's king refuse to save his own?"

"Yea, Olaf," was the reply; "Halfjord does refuse to save his own if in so doing he must grasp in good fellowship the hands of these robbers. I pray you press me no more, I would ride to see the beauteous Grunhilde and have but little time to spare for your sad fears. Olaf, you are a valiant soldier, a faithful minister, but you have been so long enveloped in the clouds of statecraft that your clear vision has lost its penetration and you have naught for our ears save tidings of storms which never break."

"Thou sayest true, king," impetuously interrupted the young man. "'Storms which never break'—why break they not? Because Olaf, seeing them afar, hath warned thee and till now thou hast heard my warnings, but now dost thou turn

thine ear from me.   Oh! Halfjord, if now
thou refusest to hearken unto me such a
storm shall sweep over thy kingdom as
may rend in twain the rock whereon rest-
eth thy throne!"

The king had grown impatient.   "Then
let the storm come," he replied, "but this
I say unto you, Olaf—before the King of
Landsvag will take in friendliness the
hands of these knaves who prey upon our
borders Halfjord will himself lead his
troops against Harold and all who come
with him, and if the heart of Olaf trem-
bleth at such thought let him remain to
guard her who shall soon be Landsvag's
queen."

At this covert imputation of cowardice
Olaf flashed up like a train of powder.
"Thou sayest cruel things unto Olaf, king,
but hear this before I go: thou hast sealed
the doom of thy land and of thy throne,
but before Landsvag falls shall Olaf go
down fighting for the land of his fathers
and, when thou hast been bereft of thy
crown and eatest the bread of a menial,

then shalt thou remember the words of Olaf and grieve thee over Olaf's death!"

He turned to go, but the king called him back. "You are over-hasty, Olaf; I know full well your devotion, nor do I doubt your courage, but that you ask of me King of Landsvag may never do. Go, tell Jorg he hath too timid fancies and bid him remain for our nuptials; go, good Olaf, I am weary of these heavy affairs and would rest."

As Olaf passed out from the king's presence he met Jorg who, alive to the exigencies of the situation, was waiting him at every turn.

"What news?" he asked as he stepped to Olaf's side. "Shall I ride today to seal the doom of this Harold?"

"Not today Jorg. Come with me," was Olaf's reply as he led the way to the cabinet where he had first received the old baron. When they were alone the old man crossed his arms over his bosom and asked: "What of Landsvag?"

"How mean you, Jorg?"

"Will our land be prey to Harold?"

"Nay, if Harold seeks to take this land then must he fight."

"Olaf, you but play with me; what hath the king said?"

"The king requesteth that Jorg remain for his approaching nuptials."

"That will Jorg not do. If I may not be of service to Landsvag yet may I protect my own lands, and this day I return, but Olaf, if ever Landsvag needeth help you know where Jorg may be found."

"Yea, Jorg, if all the men of this land were but as you I should not fear to meet even the dread Harold. Go you at once?"

"My horse even now awaiteth me."

"I pray you, Jorg, send me messengers, trusty men who will bear the tidings of the day as they come to you."

"That will I, Olaf," and the two men parted with mutual expressions of esteem.

Scarcely had Jorg left the chamber when Olaf, looking out of the window, beheld Halfjord with a brilliant cavalcade ride forth on his visit to his inamorata and even as the young man with frowning

brow and compressed lips watched the
careless pleasure-seekers he saw pass
through the same gate the faithful Jorg,
attended by but a single squire. Olaf's
eyes followed Jorg, nor did he leave his
post as long as the two horsemen were in
sight. Jorg was angered and rode with
savage speed, so that Olaf could not watch
him long.

The king returned in the evening and
Olaf, going to meet him, met also Alric,
whose temper was still none of the best.
Halfjord soon retired to his chambers, first
inviting his butterfly gentlemen to meet
him at the board later. Olaf was left
alone with this giddy, fawning crowd.
Alric approached the minister.

"Olaf speaketh hot words in presence
of our king," he said; " Will Olaf dare re-
peat them now ? "

A crowd gathered around them, and in
the crowd Olaf saw scarcely a friendly eye,
but, immovable as a rock, he stood facing
his angry antagonist, just as determined to
avoid trouble as the other was to force it.
"Alric," he replied, "Olaf saith that he

thinketh, nor doth he think less than he
saith ; if Olaf's words are unkind to your
ears it were better you should close your
ears."

Olaf's cool dignity, combined with his
evident disdain, were ill-suited to an
amicable understanding between the two
and Alric broke out : " Alric closeth not
his ears to insult, nor may even the mighty
Olaf speak words that please me not ex-
cept at point of his sword ; come, Sir Min-
ister, draw and let these pretty blades say
which of us be right," and, suiting the
action to the word, Alric placed himself
on guard, but Olaf made no move to draw
his weapon. He stood for a moment un-
decided, and then in slow, measured tones
replied : "At another time, Alric, would it
greatly please me to do that you ask, and
I shall later hold you to this your chal-
lenge, but now it doth seem to me that
Landsvag hath need of all her valiant men,
and that she may not lose your estimable
services I would postpone our meeting
until that time our enemies are laid low."

Alric, seeing around him a crowd of

smiling courtiers, and enraged at Olaf's cool reception of his challenge, lost his head ; advancing, he struck Olaf full in the face with the flat of his sword, at the same time hissing between his teeth the word, "Coward !" Forth from its scabbard leaped the patriot's pure blade ; a feint, a parry, a thrust, and before the onlookers were well aware what had happened the luckless Alric lay weltering in his blood before them. Olaf stooped and wiped his sword on the skirts of the wounded man's garment, saying as he rose, "Ye are witnesses he brought this on himself." The wound proved not to be dangerous and Alric was around again not many days after the encounter, but that sword-thrust was one of those little things which change the destinies of the world.

The next day the king, angered at Olaf's wounding of his favorite, refused to receive his minister and the latter rode alone to his estate, where Grunhilde waited the day that should make her queen. Olaf paid his respects to the king's betrothed, receiving from his old-time playmate a most cordial welcome, but it was noticed that he sought the society of Grunhilde less than he did that of her companion, the lovely Hilda. He remained some days in his castle, and when he once more turned his face toward Halfjord's court he bore with him as a precious talisman Hilda's sweet promise to share his lot. Is it strange that Olaf rode with merry mind, with valiant heart, to his king's stronghold? A timid, shrinking maiden is seemingly the daintiest, yes, the weakest, of God's creatures, yet is it easier for man to storm a frowning battery of bristling guns, belching forth their iron hail of death, than to breathe into her expectant ears the tale she so loves to hear.

Shame and pride are both estranged from the heart of him who, having conquered a lovely maid, feels not that he has brought the world beneath his feet; man knows no triumph half so sweet as that of love, nor has the trump of victory a note so rich as the softly whispered consent of Love's queen. The wreath of laurel decking the victor's brow may fade, ambition's cup too oft enjoyed grow bitter to the taste,. but woman's love, the richest crown that man may wear, grows never dim while the rude hand of sorrow seemingly gilds that self-same crown with finer lustre as the rare treasures of a love not finite in its source, scarce short of infinite in its scope, shines brightly forth, illumining the dark and gloomy shadows which cast their deepening shades athwart life's pathway.

Man, working with a shapeless lump of clay, produces beauteous forms in counterfeit of life; Nature, in her wondrous workshop, transforms the lustreless carbon into the flashing gem ; but, most marvelous of all, the Creator fashions from the dust our feet have spurned his masterpiece, woman, and, breathing into her the breath of life, sets upon her heart the seal of divinity — love — for " God is love," and love is woman's being.

As the clay takes shape beneath the sculptor's hand, so does man's oft rude embrace awake to endless life this sleeping divinity of her soul, and, yet, lovely as woman's love is at all times, it is as the

uncut gem until the sharp blade of afflic-
tion brings forth the hidden light that then
flashes from her pure soul to light the
weary way of grateful man.

Not all the praise of man is half so rich
as the willing homage of her heart, nor all
the hidden treasures in the mighty hills of
earth so great wealth as her loving, trust-
ing smile — that smile, that glance, which,
freely given, may yet not be bought.
Woman may sell herself, but she cannot
sell her heart, and he who has won that
heart has life's rarest prize. Let him
guard it carefully, nurture it tenderly; let
him reverently uncover his head, for in the
atmosphere of her pure love he stands in
the very presence of his God.

The young man, happy in acknowledged,
triumphant love, rode, as we have said,
gayly singing, dreaming, a thousand fond
fancies filling his active brain; as far as he
could see had he gazed back at the gloomy
walls of that castle, watching a white ker-
chief fluttering in the breeze. He could
see the little rag long after the arm that
held it was lost to view, but now neither

could be seen, not even the frowning out-
lines of the building itself, and he must
content himself with memories and dreams.
He rode hard. Affairs of state had now
no place in his heart, except that he
thought them cruel disturbers of love's
first sweet joys. He sought the court that
he might know what had transpired, do
what was required, and then return to his
love—this the reason he spurred his horse
almost cruelly—every hour's delay on the
road was an hour longer from Hilda's side,
and he had told her he would be absent
but a day. But a day! How little we know
of the morrow's fate. Grunhilde was queen,
and Hilda's cheeks had grown pale with
fear, her eyes dim from tears, before that
promised morrow came.

It was evening when Olaf drew rein in
the courtyard of Halfjord's castle, and, as
he sprang from his horse, a young man
respectfully saluted him. He started with
surprise, exclaiming: "What, Jegge!
Whence come you, boy, and where is your
father — here ?"

"Jorg is not here," the young man

gravely answered. " I come to Olaf from him."

" Bear you a message from him, Jegge ? "

" Yea, for your ears, alone."

"Follow me, then," and Olaf, without waiting upon the king or even sending a message to announce his return, showed the way at once to his private chamber. For a long time the two men were closeted, and when he emerged it was with a troubled brow that Olaf went at once to the king's presence.

Halfjord was surrounded, as usual, with his favorites. Olaf was known to be in disgrace temporarily, and his entry was the signal for many sly winks and whispered jests, but, as he strode toward the king there was that in his face which warned the boldest to have a care for himself.

"So, Sir Swordspoint, you have returned ?"

"Yea, King Halfjord, I have returned from paying my devotions to the lovely Grunhilde, who honoreth the walls of Olaf's home, that she doth shelter herself within them till thou shalt take her thence."

Halfjord was in love, Halfjord was also generous ; the man who had just returned from a visit to the expected queen could not longer be the victim of his temper. He spoke heartily : "There Olaf did well; and how fareth our sweet Grunhilde ?"

"Well, king ; never hath she been lovelier than when she spoke of thee and whispered sweet messages I should bear thee."

Halfjord's eyes glistened.   "And the messages, Olaf ?"

"Are for thine own ear, king."

"Yet you bear them."

"Is not Grunhilde's foster-brother Olaf fit messenger unto Grunhilde's chosen lover Halfjord ?" was the reply.

"True, Olaf, we will hear these honeyed words for which our heart doth hunger. Attend me, Olaf — wait us here" (addressing the crowd).

Olaf followed the king, carefully closed the door and when they were alone abruptly said, "Halfjord, I lied to thee." The king stared at him in unfeigned astonishment, but the young man went on.

"I lied and that lie was for Landsvag's sake and for Halfjord's throne. There is that I must tell thee this night, yet had I not spoken Grunhilde's name thou wouldst have turned me off as before and sought thy more pleasing companions. My king may refuse to forgive the lie but my friend Halfjord will not."

Halfjord had already grown sulky at thought of being entrapped into a business interview, but Olaf's closing appeal woke the sleeping magnanimity of his soul. He took Olaf's hand familiarly and said half reproachfully, "You played me a sorry trick, Olaf, but you have me now; I will hear you."

"Both as king and brother, Halfjord?"

"Yea, Olaf, my heart is ever with you, though I love not work and give my smiles to those who help me play."

"Even they will need to work now, Halfjord."

"Wherefore?"

"King, the barons I would have had thee join as against Harold have been dashed to pieces against the rocky wall of

his mighty army, their lands despoiled and
Harold advances with none to oppose him
upon our Landsvag."

"Who bringeth such dark news ?"

"It cometh from Jorg by his son Jegge."

"Jorg ? Is he not here ? "

" Nay, king, he loves his land more than
he fears thy displeasure and though bid-
den to await thy nuptials he returned
home that he might watch like a faithful
sentinel."

" He was right," said the king thought-
fully, then added, "What would you that
we do, Olaf ?"

"There is naught left but to put all
Landsvag against this man who seeks to
enslave us."

"Nay, Olaf, war hath a cruel sound to
him who seeks the soft delights of love."

" Hath it so cruel a sound, Halfjord, as
slavery ? "

" Nay, my good Olaf, but I would have
neither.   At another time when sweet
Grunhilde's eyes are less bright will we
take the field against this knave, but not
now, Olaf, not now."

"Shall he then take from thee thy kingdom that thou mayest take and enjoy this maiden?" exclaimed Olaf angrily.

"Not so, Olaf, Halfjord will have the maiden but Harold shall have not this throne."

"What meanest thou, king?"

"This, Olaf: You shall go to this Harold, make peace with him on terms not beneath our dignity; when he hath gone his way then shall we rise against him, bind to us these border barons and overturn his sway."

"Thy words have good and pleasant sound, king, but Harold makes no peace."

"He will with the valiant Olaf."

The interview was prolonged into the night, Halfjord insisting, Olaf objecting; the king, of course, had his way and just before dawn Olaf, Jegge and two faithful squires rode forth to the east, which is why Grunhilde was queen before Hilda's morrow came.

CHAPTER IV

Harold, "the Fair-haired," full of the venturesome spirit of this age of the Vikings, sought to put all Norway under his rule, and through the land his victorious army had advanced, leaving in its wake dethroned kings, obliterated principalities, death and devastation; whether singly or leagued together, the petty sovereigns who disputed his way shared the same fate — defeat — and those to whom the god of war was so unkind as to spare their lives found themselves unwilling vassals to this terrible scourge who swept everything before him.

The law of compensation is inevitable, immutable; no evil exists without its correlative good and yet, while admitting this, we find it but cold comfort if it so happens that the evil comes to us in order that unborn generations may reap the harvest of good.

The French revolution, with all its sickening horrors, was not unmitigated evil; since, for every bloody head that rolled its reeking way from the hissing blade of the guillotine into the sawdust-filled basket, another head, living and moving, has been raised from the pestilential slime of despotism's dungeon into the living light of liberty.   But still, to the headless trunk, the trunkless head or the force-freed soul that sped from the guillotine platform to —where ?—the knife which pruned the too luxuriant branches of the tree of royalty and unearned privilege that through the gap might shine the noonday beams of the sun of freedom was but the cursed agent of despair.

Were it not for the hideous spectres of our own griefs which, with rude persistence, ever sit as guests at banquet table or stalk in frightful silence by our sides, this house of earth were much too fair a home; but for the compensating good bequeathed by those before us, a legacy of tears and blood to them, this home of earth were but a gruesome charnel-house, at every step a grinning skeleton of dead hopes, murdered joys, our only light as we grope our stumbling way the fitful phosphorescent gleam from their sightless sockets.

The tears of our ancestors water the soil from which springs the bountiful harvest of our happiness, while from the rolling tide of their joys rise the silent vapors which, condensing into clouds of sorrow, pour down a tempest of tears upon our troubled souls.

Thus Harold was a scourge—the Lord's scourge—and indeed 'twas cruel to the victims, but the Almighty works in His own way; God's sword was in Harold's hand, though the despoiler knew it not and in his blindness dreamt he worked but for his own ends. Through the glass of history we can see those things which from their clouded eyes were hid—each briny tear that fell from woman's swimming eyes, the silent token of a bruised and broken heart, beneath the magic touch of time became a priceless pearl in Norway's diadem; each drop of blood that welled from patriot's heart in the Divine

Alchemist's hands has long since been transformed into one link of an endless chain of love, soft as the gossamer thread of a spider's web, yet binding as the hardest steel, welding together in indissoluble union a people whose curses of ten centuries ago, drifting on through limitless space, have reached the heavenly orchestra and now sweep back to earth, their harsh notes mellowed into the soft cadences of life's sweetest symphony, awaking the universe to tuneful harmony.

So it was that Harold, in all the pride of his greatness, stood, one night shortly after the events just related, surveying the mighty host encamped around him as he conversed with his chief lieutenant.

"What land lieth there, Eric?" he asked, stretching his arm toward where the gloomy outline of a range of hills was just discernible on the night sky.

"Beyond those hills is Landsvag, king."

"Ah! the land of Halfjord, he who loves his ease; 'twill be an easy prey, Eric."

"Not so, king."

"Not so? Why?"

"Harold, the King of Landsvag, takes his ease because he hath Olaf; the king sleeps but Olaf takes no sleep; Halfjord plays but Olaf works; the king makes merry while the man does watch; while Olaf fights Halfjord dances; while Halfjord rests Olaf rules."

"Who is this Olaf of whom you speak? Methinks I have heard the name, yet doth my memory fail me."

"Olaf, king, is the thunderbolt of Landsvag; though still a mere youth yet doth he with his single arm support the throne his old father established. Leader in the field, ruler in the closet, he unites all factions; some cling to him for love of him, others for fear because he crushes those who oppose him even as thou wouldst the worm beneath thy heel. A valiant warrior who leads a host of mighty men, he will meet thee face to face, Harold, and though thou shalt conquer this land as thou hast all others yet will Olaf make it cost thee much blood."

"In good sooth, Eric," said Harold, "you make me to love this man Olaf from very sound of his deeds. I will, myself, cross blades with this famous warrior when we do meet him."

"Oh, king, I beseech thee, seek not this Olaf on the field ; those who know do say that in battle he is a very demon and even the bravest go down before him, for none may withstand the fierce Olaf."

"Ah ! Eric, now speak you unto my own heart, for none may withstand Harold ; if none may withstand Olaf why then are we giants in battle and well matched; verily, I will meet this wizard of Landsvag; nay, even more—by all the gods of our race ! if I had him here I would play him the pretty game of single combat, his land against mine to be the stakes. Eric, my hand tingles to match blades with so doughty a foe. I will—"

But the sentence was not finished. A commotion arose a short distance from them and an officer approaching hurriedly with evident signs of excitement spoke without waiting to be addressed: "King, a man from Landsvag seeks audience with thee ; he says he comes with a message from Halfjord and would deliver unto thee alone."

"What manner of man is he, Hengis?" asked the king.

"Of fine presence and lordly bearing, king—a soldier of tried mettle if I mistake not."

"We will see him; bid him here, Hengis." As the officer moved away to execute the king's order the latter turned to Eric and said, half playfully: "A pleasing fancy hath hold of my mind, Eric—what if this messenger were your own doughty Olaf?"

"Halfjord might not trust his most mighty leader in thy hands, Harold."

"I know not; Halfjord doth know we make war as men and destroy not those who come unto us in peace with fair words on their tongues."

Eric shook his head, saying, as he peered into the distance: "Thou shalt soon know ; here cometh him who would speak with thee."

"Then bid them bring lights that we may see the face of him who beareth Halfjord's message."

Olaf, with young Jegge, had ridden first to Jorg's castle and, leaving his son to guard their home, Jorg had joined Olaf. Together they entered the enemy's camp; they were surrounded and after stating their mission held until Harold gave orders to have them brought to him.

Eric soon had a number of torches burning around the king's quarters, their fitful, ruddy glow, painfully suggestive of the blood that had been shed by these rude warriors, combined with the black and swarthy forms that moved to and fro amid the lurid glare, suggesting to the minds of the approaching emissaries a carnival of some of the most dreaded demons of their mythology.

Olaf, Jorg and the two squires, the latter leading the horses, approached dismounted; the escort, as they neared the spot where the king stood, separated and passing around on both sides left the four in the centre of an open space in which

beside themselves the king alone stood.
As the four drew near, their guard, in con-
junction with those around the king,
crowded in behind, forming a circle of
solid steel, a chain with not a broken
link.

Olaf and Jorg had something of an ad-
vantage at the start — Harold was ignorant
of their names as well as of their mission,
while they, already knowing their errand,
no sooner beheld that giant frame topped
with a luxuriant mass of tawny curls falling
over his shoulders like the sunlit ripples
of an unruly stream than they knew in
whose presence they stood.

Approaching within a few feet, the two
men saluted the king with dignified re-
spect. He returned the salute, following
it with a gesture that stopped them where
they stood.

"Who be ye," he asked, "that, strangers,
yet seek the camp of Harold ?"

"We are of Landsvag, King Harold,"
replied Olaf, quietly, "and bear thee a
message from our good King Halfjord."

"That hath been already told," was the

king's answer. " But before we hear the message you bring to us we would know with whom we speak."

Olaf raised his head and in the proud, half-challenging poise of that head was a majesty that not even kings may borrow —the majesty of a pure, irreproachable soul that, forced to dwell for a time within these thralling walls of weak and perishable clay, yet never yields so completely to the bondage of this flesh as to lose entirely the impress of the seal of divinity; he lifted his arm and, pointing to his companion, said : " King Harold, those gray hairs with which these night winds so carelessly disport themselves do crown a head that hath never yet bowed in weak submission to victorious foe, nor yet hath harbored thought of treason to acknowledged king ; here standeth a man who hath bared his breast to storm of war that kings might be made ; again, that those made might be saved, and yet hath never sought of those his arm upheld the smallest boon.   In homage to his rightful king he bends a willing knee, but that selfsame knee hath not yet learned the fawning crook of servile sycophancy! Look around thee, King Harold, and see if among thy bold and valiant men thou hast one so faithful unto thee as Jorg, Baron of Norges, is to Halfjord of Landsvag. As to myself, I am called Olaf."

Jorg would have spoken, but Harold silenced him with a gesture, as he said : "There be many Olafs ; are you Olaf of Landsvag, old Morgen's son ?"

"Yea, king ; Morgen was my father."

Harold regarded the young man with a half-curious, half-respectful look, but, after a moment's silence, he called out, "Eric ! come hither ; behold Olaf of Landsvag, who putteth himself in Harold's hands !"

Eric, however, was a doubter. He came at the king's call, and, carefully scanning the young man who stood before him, said : "How know we, king, that this man is he whom he claims to be ? It were more likely that he cometh with foul purpose, and the better to accomplish his end taketh the name of Olaf."

"Yet hath he a soldier's bearing."

"Yea, king, and a brave front, but Eric believeth not that Olaf of Landsvag cometh unto Harold; wouldst thou send Eric unto Halfjord?"

"Nay; for Eric might not return."

"Even so then Halfjord sendeth not Olaf unto Harold for fear he returneth not."

The king, half doubting, more than half believing, mused for a while, but when he again raised his head and looked at Olaf, the young man's gallant bearing and apparent sincerity, coupled with old Jorg's evident respect for his companion, seemed to decide him—he turned to Eric and said: "Yon gray head hath a noble air, methinks it truckleth not to traitor nor yet to assassin. See, we will prove their truth. If this be the great Olaf, Harold will make him prick up his ears." Then turning to the two men waiting before him the king exclaimed: "Now, thanks be to Thor, who hath so soon granted Harold's wish; this very night, hearing of the deeds of Olaf, Harold did sigh for sight of this man who, having made a throne, refused it and gave to his friends that which he himself had earned. Nay, more, Harold even said that were Olaf to come unto him he would himself draw sword in single combat, the gage to be Landsvag against Harold's vast domain — what say you, Olaf ?"

The young man's eyes flashed ; instinctively his hand sought his sword as he replied : " King Harold, Olaf would gladly engage thee ; nor doth the charger leap so lightly 'neath his rider's spur as would Olaf's sword when Harold gave the word. For thy dominions care I naught ; let the gage be Landsvag free if Olaf wins, and then, with kind permission of my good King Halfjord, will I before thy great army with this strong arm maintain even to thy face, great king, the glory of my native land !"

Harold had watched him closely during this speech, and at its close, advancing, he threw one arm around the speaker, and raising the other exclaimed : " Behold a foe in whom Harold delighteth ! Verily, this is

Olaf, for none other would dare to brave in mortal combat Harold, the scourge of the Northland. Olaf, foe or friend, Harold greets you, for Harold loves a man who is a man ! "

Olaf, taken by surprise, hardly knew what to say, but gathering himself together he answered : " King, thy words please Olaf, yet have I words for thee from Half-jord which I would fain speak in thine own ear."

"Not tonight, good Olaf ; you and your faithful companions shall even lodge this night with Harold ; on the morrow will we hear what your king hath to say."

At this Eric whispered : " King, beware how thou receivest those whom thou knowest not !" But Harold, seeming not to hear this warning, dismissed the gathered crowd and led the way to his tent, leaving none outside save his usual guard.

Olaf, a bit skeptical as to Harold's sincerity, as well as impatient to return, seemed not to fully appreciate his generous reception. He said nothing, but a close observer might have noted both his wary watchfulness and his restlessness. On the other hand, Harold, delighted at the chance which gave him an opportunity of entertaining the man who, next to himself, was most famous in Norway, and, feeling irresistibly attracted by Olaf's blunt and fearless honesty, was loath to see the time come when the young emissary would turn his face homeward.

In the morning all of Harold's leaders were called to breakfast with his visitors, and, following their king's example, they sought in every way to allay suspicions which the two men might still harbor, yet through the whole meal Olaf's quick eye was on the alert for any unexpected move.

It was high noon before, after repeated solicitation on Olaf's part, the king, leaving Jorg at table with the others, repaired to his tent to receive from Olaf Halfjord's message. Just as they rose Eric said: "King, it is not prudent to trust thyself alone with an avowed enemy."

Olaf's cheek flushed; drawing his sword he offered it to Eric saying: "Olaf is no assassin, but if Eric hath such evil thoughts let him keep this sword that he may not fear for Harold's safety."

"Nay, nay, Olaf," said the king, "none think so harshly of you nor shall any hold your sword; Harold is content nor feareth evil. Eric, your zeal for your king putteth hot words in your mouth."

Entering the tent Harold asked : " What hath Halfjord to say unto Harold ?"

" King, Halfjord saith war is cruel, and war when it be not necessary a crime ; if thou shouldst force him Halfjord will meet thee with a powerful army, and each step thou takest shall be over the bodies of the slain ; but Halfjord, King of Landsvag, offereth thee friendship for enmity, peace for war, life for death — wilt thou take it, king, or art thou so wedded unto the rude art of war as to spurn the gentle presence of peace ? "

" Harold hath no great love for war, nor hath he ever yet refused to hear those who would, for sake of peace, submit to his rule. If Halfjord hath desire to offer allegiance it pleases me."

"Submit! Offer allegiance!" fairly gasped Olaf. "Good king, you jest."

"I jest not, Olaf."

"Hath Harold so mean opinion of the King of Landsvag as to think he yields his crown without a blow? Know this, oh I mighty Harold—thou dealest not with so cowardly a king, nor, if the King of Landsvag had so craven a heart, would Olaf bear his message so foul. I come to offer thee a fair and honorable alliance, king, but naught beyond that save the war thy rude refusal shall force upon us. We seek not to grasp that which is not ours, but that which is shall we hold with firm hand, and it needeth a long arm and heavy sword to wrest it from our grasp. King, shall Halfjord meet thee with uplifted sword or with the outstretched hand of friendship? It is for thee to say—what answer shall Olaf bear unto Halfjord?"

"That if he acknowledge us he may hold his lands, his kingship, a fief under our good pleasure; if this he refuse, then shall we take from him both lands and throne."

"If this thy answer to the friendly offers

of Halfjord, then hear me, king, as I hurl thy threats back into thy teeth.   For every step thou takest beyond yon hills, that mark the line of Halfjord's kingdom, an hundred of thy warriors shall die; the rivers thou wouldst drink from shall run red as wine with the blood of thy slain, and when thou wouldst rest thee thy couch shall be the putrid corpse of one of these, thy followers, who now raise aloft their heads in such lusty pride; thus, proud king, doth Landsvag meet those who come with arms in their hands."

Harold had listened with a half-amused smile playing around his lips as the young man delivered this challenge, and when he paused for breath the king said: "You are bold of speech, and yet your words please me ; my heart rejoiceth in a valiant man, even though he be Harold's foe."

"Not bolder in word than in deed, king, as thou shalt find when thou shalt cross yon hills ; Olaf will meet thee at head of Landsvag's troops.   Did I but venture my life thou shouldst have that meeting thou sayest thou cravest, but without Halfjord's permission I may not stake his kingdom upon the prick of a sword; yet, though I may not now accept thy challenge, look to thyself, oh, king! when the battle joins, for Olaf will search thee out, and, finding thee, the issue shall be not a kingdom but thy life or mine."

"Verily," said Harold, "you speak harsh words to one who can, with one word, turn that manly body into carrion. Nay, nay, Olaf, think not so hardly of Harold," he broke in, as the young man at the implied threat laid his hand on his sword in evidence that he would sell his life dearly, "you are Harold's guest, and on Harold's honor shall have safe conduct through this camp; Harold will gladly meet you, and when you seek him it shall not be in vain. See, I will wear this scarf that you may the more readily know me — but Harold, like Olaf, is no assassin." Under sudden impulse the king sprang forward, reaching forth his hand as he said: "Come, brave Olaf, we must fight, for Landsvag must be mine; but I love your noble heart, and while you tarry with me I would you were my friend; your hand, good Olaf; let it be good fellowship now, though no quarter when on the field we meet."

Olaf grasped the proffered hand, saying : "Thou art a brave and generous foe ; my heart leaps with joy at thought of meeting thee in combat, and yet thou wouldst be better friend than enemy. I grieve that thou shouldst force upon us this coming slaughter — have we no way to peace, king?"

"Yea, that which I have named."

"No more, I pray thee ; thy offer repeated insults my ears. My mission here is ended ; I fain would leave thee, king, and when again thou seest me 'twill be the last time, even as this is the first."

"Though I would have you with us longer," replied the king, "yet is Olaf's wish Harold's command. If it be your wish to go, Harold himself will see you safe outside our camp;" and the king started to lead the way outside, but Olaf, seemingly clinging to the last straw, said : "King, hast thou naught else to say unto Halfjord ?"

"Naught, Olaf," answered Harold without so much as turning around, "save that which hath been said." Olaf made no reply but followed the king.

Curious eyes were fastened on these two men who held, as it were, the destinies of kingdoms within their grasp, as they rejoined the merry circle without; Jorg raised his eyes to Olaf's face, saw and understood; a glance was sufficient for the old warhorse; that mysterious keen sympathy of soul had told him before he looked that their mission had been fruitless; on the other hand, Harold's officers knowing nothing, surmised much and, when Harold on returning seemed even more gracious than before, they believed that Landsvag had yielded without so much as a blow. But this idea was dispelled before it had time to take definite shape. Harold, as soon as they reached the crowd, called out : "Now, Olaf, before you leave us one merry toast ! "

" And that toast, king ? " was the quiet query.

" To Olaf, the fearless warrior of Landsvag." Olaf replied with quiet dignity: "That toast I may not drink, but I drink with thee to Landsvag first—may she ever be free ; then to Harold, a brave soldier, a knightly foe, a generous king—may he rule long over the lands he holdeth, but not over Landsvag ! "

Harold laughed while his lieutenants with gloomy brows and half-suppressed mutterings listened to this bold challenge. "Of a truth, Olaf," said the amused king, "you have a faithful heart but hold too loose a rein upon your tongue to speak in presence of your enemies. You offer me a toast to mine own undoing, yet will I drink with you, for in a glass of wine lieth naught but good fellowship." Then lifting his goblet he cried out: "Ho! to Olaf's toast !"

Harold, Olaf and Jorg drank alone this strange toast. "Bring forth the horses !" then cried Harold, "We will ride with Olaf and Jorg toward Landsvag."

Harold's free and easy treatment of his formidable foe met but little favor with his generals, all of whom stood by with sullen countenances and gathered here and there in little knots, voicing their displeasure in undertones; at last, just before the party was ready to mount, Eric left one of these disaffected groups and, approaching Harold, said in an undertone: "King, we beseech thee, let not Olaf return."

"Wherefore, Eric?"

"In so doing thou puttest into the hands of thy most powerful enemy a weapon."

"Not so, Eric, by kindness I disarm him; but even if that you say be true Harold maketh not war against him who cometh with open hands; Olaf hath our kingly word and we will see that he cometh to no harm through us. Let us mount and away," and Harold vaulted into the saddle, leading the way with Olaf and Jorg on either side of him.

Harold's officers rode clustered around Eric some distance in the rear. "What said the king when you spoke unto him,

Eric?" asked a fierce, bearded giant as he pressed the powerful stallion he strode close in against Eric's horse.

"Why, the same smooth answer that Harold ever gives," was the reply.

"And doth he mean that Olaf shall depart?"

"Yea, Rolje, he saith his kingly word is pledged."

Others crowded closer around to hear what was said. "He may depart but why should he reach Halfjord?" asked one.

"What mean you, Hengis?" inquired Rolje.

"What mean I? It seemeth easy enough unto Hengis. The king's permission for a foray secured, one of us taketh an hundred trusty men and making after this Olaf we slay him; it were for our good and the king need never know it was we who killed Olaf."

"Hengis, thou hast hit upon a happy plan; I will gain the king's consent. Now who shall lead in this pretty plot?"

No one spoke for a time. Eric's question had brought the point close home;

none of them feared the outcome so far as Olaf was concerned, but all dreaded the king's anger should he find out what they had done.   Finally Rolje said, "I will do it, Eric."

"Ride back then, Rolje, and pick your men.   Stay; on second thought it were best not to take so many ; they are but four, a score will do the work as well and talk less."

Rolje galloped back toward the camp, while the rest, their spirits heightened since the hatching of their plot, rode on in the wake of their king.

Reaching the outpost Harold stopped, and, holding out a hand to each of the two men, said, "We part here, to meet again on the field of battle.   Harold will have Landsvag, but Harold grieveth that ye are not with him.   Verily, Olaf, I love you, though I shall kill you when again we meet."

"King Harold, I thank thee for thy kind attention ; it seemeth pity we should be foes, but being foes I scarce can wait the day when this good sword of mine

shall cross with thine. Thou sayest thou
wilt kill me—beware, king, lest Olaf's
blade drink thy own hot blood. Until
thou facest Halfjord's army farewell,
king!" And doffing his cap Olaf spurred
forward, followed closely by Jorg and their
squires.

A few hundred yards away was a slight
knoll, and, reaching the top, Olaf wheeled,
faced the camp, and, drawing his sword,
waved it as though in challenge. As he
did so Eric rode to the king's side and
said : "King, Rolje asketh thy good con-
sent that he take men and beat up the
country ; we are in need of provisions."

"Let him go, but see that he followeth
not Olaf; I would not have harm come
unto him."

"Yea, king, it shall be done as thou
sayest," and Eric turned to a rider near him
and spoke a few words in an undertone,
whereupon the man galloped away toward
the center of the great camp.

The king musingly watched the distant
horseman and, as if speaking to himself,
said : "One such heart as his is worth to a

king a whole army." Olaf was out of
sight when the cavalcade followed Harold
back to the camp. Eric at once made in-
quiry about Rolje; learning that he had
started immediately upon receiving word
of the king's consent, Eric was content,
Hengis was happy—all save Harold were
expectant.

In the meantime Olaf and Jorg were
making the best of their time, each with
brain full of the work he knew awaited
him. Jorg had learned in a few words the
result of Olaf's mission, and was impatient
to get back that he might prepare for the
inevitable struggle; Olaf's heart, filled
with sadness at the prospect of Landsvag's
coming fiery trial, yet found room for
softer fancies as the sweet image of gentle
Hilda floated before his gaze. They had
ridden for some hours, scarce exchanging
a word, when an exclamation from their
two followers, who were some distance be-
hind, caused them to rein in. Dashing up
the man said that both he and his com-
panion had several times thought they
heard the hoofs of horses, and but a mo-

ment before they had caught sight of a body of mounted men riding hotly after them, as though in pursuit. Olaf called the other man, who verified his fellow's statement, and even as they spoke the pounding of heavy hoofs greeted their ears.

"Surely," said Olaf, "Harold is not the dastard to send a troop to strike us in the back. What think you of this, Jorg?"

"I think," was the quiet response, "we must fight."

"Ah! Harold, Harold!" exclaimed Olaf passionately, as he shook his clenched fist in the direction from which he had come, "this is a foul deed, worthy of an assassin, but not of a mighty king!"

"Harold hath not done this," said Jorg. "I am old, Olaf, and see with the eyes of age. Harold is no liar. This hath been done by those who knit their gloomy brows at us, and he knoweth it not, but we must fight if we would live."

"If it be not Harold's doing I care not," answered Olaf. "See! Let us turn into this timber for shelter, and when they have passed us, then can we catch them in the narrow pass between yon hills, where one man is even as a score."

They turned into the woods and going a short distance halted, where they might see and possibly hear all that passed though themselves well screened from view. They had waited but a few moments when Rolje dashed up at the head of his squad, some twenty strong. Drawing rein he halted almost directly opposite where the four were hidden and first closely scanning the road in his front said to his men: "We have them now; the proud Olaf cannot be much beyond that bend in the road. Harold's greatest foe is before us; let us hasten but once more let each man swear to reveal naught of that we do, for Harold's anger would strike even as the lightning from yonder sky."

"We swear!" cried the men in chorus, brandishing aloft their swords.

"Forward then! death to Olaf!"

"Death to Olaf!" echoed from lip to lip as the column dashed on.

"Heard you their words, Olaf?" asked Jorg.

"Yea, Harold hath naught with such foul carrion-seekers." Then pointing his finger after the receding column he cried: "Assassins! I will teach you what manner of man is this you seek to stab from behind! Jorg, we ride," and the young man led the way, closely followed by his three companions. A strange race—pursuers pursued; shall the victims be victors? 'Tis often so in life; he who runs is not always vanquished nor he who pursues triumphant.

As Olaf rounded the bend in the road Rolje was just nearing a rocky cut, narrow with high walls; the young man saw the column stretch out into twos and halting said: "See where they ride; they leave us room; now at them. We ride four, they ride two; forward and strike for Landsvag! Let each blow be death!" Olaf and Jorg were in the center, a squire on either side as they swept like a whirlwind against the unconscious enemy.

Rolje, having no thought of the rear, was pressing on, wondering somewhat that he came not in sight of those he sought, and slowing up to breathe his horses was just entering the narrow defile when with a shout: "Landsvag! Landsvag!" the four struck his rear with terrific force. The two horsemen who received the first shock went down before they could turn in their saddles, the next two followed; all was dire confusion—the clash of steel, oaths, imprecations; maddened horses plunging, tearing their sides against the ragged rocks. Rolje sought to wheel his men that he might face the foe but each rider as he turned found one of the four ready for him. Through the column they forced their bloody way, a terrible wedge, splitting and tearing as it drove into the heart of this quivering flesh. Nearly half of Rolje's force was down.

Olaf, now wedged in, carcasses behind, a living wall before, espied Rolje and cried out: "You who would slay Olaf come! he waits!" but Rolje, bent upon getting his men out, disregarded the challenge. There were left of his twenty twelve beside himself; four faced about, covering the retreat while the rest sought to press on beyond the binding walls of rock; a charge, two of the four went down, the others turned and fled after their comrades, close pressed by Olaf; again the shock, two more were down, eight were now left, but the road began to widen, Rolje made one last effort; wheeling, he charged himself at the head of his decimated troop. A crash, the devoted four, outnumbered, almost surrounded, recoiled; Rolje, taking advantage of this, put spurs to his horse and dashing up the steep slope that now led off from the road escaped, followed by seven of his men, but not before Olaf's sword had drank deep of his blood.

Olaf made no effort to follow the fugitives but said smilingly, as he wiped his sword on his horse's mane: "Harold will have not so many men when Landsvag meets him." Then noting that they were but three he asked: "Where is Thorsen?"

"Dead, Olaf," replied Jorg, without a sign of personal feeling, though the unhappy man had been his own faithful servant for many years.

"He was a valiant man and deserved a better fate," said Olaf.

"Yes, Olaf."

By nightfall they had reached Jorg's domains, and shortly after entered the castle. Jegge, coming forward to meet them, heard in a few words the result of the embassy, and the boy, full of the sublime confidence of youth, could scarcely conceal his delight at the prospect of war; to his mind war meant glory for his land, renown for himself; he could not understand defeat except when it overtook the enemy.

Olaf, after supping and resting for an hour, declined further hospitality, and pushed on to the court from which he had already been two weeks absent, leaving the faithful Jorg to watch the frontier until Halfjord's entire force could take the field.

That same night a weary, crestfallen band of seven, two of whom bore between them the insensible body of their leader, while a third led a riderless horse, made their way over the ragged hills that marked Landsvag's boundary. Day was breaking when they reached Harold's camp, and in whispers told the other conspirators what had befallen them. Rolje was not dead, but sorely wounded. On the third day, as Eric, Hengis and others stood around his couch, he said: "This Olaf is no man, but a demon; he slew thirteen of my bravest men and gave me this soft reminder of his visit. If Harold meets Olaf in the field he will need to call upon Thor for help."

History has never satisfactorily accounted for Harold's delay just at this juncture; he might have marched on Landsvag immediately after Olaf left him, and yet his army lay idle for ten days before the march was begun. It were a pleasing conceit that this unmilitary delay was due to a quixotic chivalry that refused to take advantage of a strategic opportunity against a worthy foe.

CHAPTER V

Olaf's absence during the festivities attending Halfjord's wedding was naturally the subject of much comment; speculation was rife as to both the occasion of his sudden departure and the nature of his secret errand. As for Grunhilde, she complained bitterly to the king of Olaf's apparent slight, seeking to draw from her spouse some information, but Halfjord held his peace, which, for a bridegroom, was a most remarkable feat, and is remembered to this day by the descendants of the men he once ruled. However, despite the king's silence, the news of Harold's approach, his victories, Landsvag's danger, began to filter through a thousand leaks; wild stories were told with bulging eyes, heard with bated breath ; an air of uncertainty, uneasiness, pervaded the court, dimming the most brilliant fetes given in

honor of the young queen.   It would have
been strange if the gossips had failed to
connect Olaf's secret departure with the
impending invasion, and they told some
stories hitting marvellously near the real
truth.   The fever of excitement grew, new
reports came daily, hourly, from the fron-
tier, and still Olaf came not.

After the interview with Hilda already
related, Olaf went at once to greet the re-
turning king.   As the gay cavalcade, cur-
veting and prancing, entered the court-
yard, the sight of Olaf awaiting them
produced intense excitement.   Halfjord,
leaping from his horse, extended his hand
as he said :   "Olaf, we welcome you; your
presence maketh now our new joy com-
plete."

Olaf bowed, saying in a low tone:
"King, I thank thee.   I have much for
thine own ear."

"I will summon you shortly," replied
his sovereign.

A gallant-looking young fellow, hand-
some, magnificently attired, one of whom
we shall see more, sprang toward Olaf and,

clapping him familiarly on the shoulder, said: "You have missed much merry sport, Olaf."

"Yea, Erling," was the quiet response, "but Olaf hath seen much merry sport."

"Yet do you bear a sorry countenance for one who taketh life's pleasures."

"'Tis but the dust of travel, Erling; I I will go prepare for the night. What pleasing fancy hath the king for this night's diversion?"

"A great dinner, at which both we and our fair ladies shall be present."

"It is well; I shall be there," and he left the crowd.

"What saith our lordly Olaf, Erling?" asked Alric.

"He saith he will dine with the king to-night, Alric."

"Ah! But his sour face will make but sorry pleasantry."

"Nay, Alric, Olaf hath not so black a face," said one, while another laughingly cried: "No, but with Olaf at the board Alric's hand will so itch for his sword that it may spill the cup of wine. Eh, Alric?" This reference to the recent encounter, from the effects of which Alric was just recovering, provoked a general laugh at his expense as the group dispersed.

Olaf responded at once when the king sent to bid him come. Halfjord seemed deeply concerned and plied the young man with questions, readily and promptly answered. He had never seemed to Olaf so nearly what a king should be, and when, after hearing of Harold's cool statement that Landsvag should be his, the king burst forth indignantly : "Not while Halfjord sits upon its throne!" Olaf threw his arms about him as he said : "There spoke my king! Halfjord, thou hast awakened, thy sturdy soul is roused ; now art thou indeed a king!"

"Yea, Olaf, Halfjord is King of Landsvag, and that will we show unto this Harold they call The Fair-haired. What! he will take Landsvag ? By the great Odin! Halfjord will himself take the field against this bragging knave!" Reaching out he grasped Olaf's hand as he continued : "Halfjord and Olaf — we will ride together

to meet this rude Harold. Landsvag is
the prize, lad!"

"Yea, king, and with our own Halfjord
in the field there be none in all Landsvag
will stay behind. Ah! Harold, Harold!
Look to thyself now!"

"Yea, Harold!" cried the enraged king,
"we will feed thy mighty men unto the
beasts of the forests! But, Olaf, there re-
mains much to do; our warriors must be
gathered together; we may not sit in
quietude till he disturb our rest."

"All hath been done, king," replied
Olaf; "Jorg is even now abroad keeping
watchful eye upon our border, and I have
sent messengers into every part of thy
kingdom. Before another sun shall set
thou wilt see the first gathering of a mighty
army beneath the walls of thy castle."

"Verily, Olaf, you are a wizard, naught
may be done if you do it not." And the
king bent a fond, admiring gaze on his
boyhood's companion, then added: "See-
ing that your work is done you will join
us in our last fete this night, eh, Olaf?"

"Yea, king, Olaf will be there."

Rude, half-barbarous, yet gorgeous in its very rudeness was the scene in Halfjord's banquet hall as Olaf entered shortly after leaving the king ; bright-eyed women sat beside fierce-bearded men, soft hands brushed against hard and heavy-hilted swords, while half-smothered sighs of love mingled with coarse oaths and boisterous laughter.   Great torches shed a flickering, half-uncanny light over the vast apartment whose cavernous walls seemed to mark the confines of another world.

The feast began.   All sat at one great table, Halfjord at the end, Grunhilde on his right, Olaf to the left ; further down near the center sat Hilda next to Alric, while just opposite was a young woman of unusual beauty, another of the queen's ladies, Olga by name.   The latter seemed not to like too well the arrangement at the board and sought in vain to chain the glance of Alric's vagrant eye, while Hilda, unable even to see Olaf from where she was placed, sat silent, with the air of a martyr, giving no heed to the rough courtesies of Alric.

Grunhilde was beaming, Halfjord delighted, Olaf gracious and, taking their cue from their sovereigns, the rest of the party overflowed with merriment; wild jests, hoarse shouts, mingled with shrill exclamations chasing in perfect pandemonium up and down the board.

Halfjord drank less heavily than his wont, Olaf scarce at all, but both seemed anxious to press the cup upon the others until, at a signal from Olaf, who feared a too speedy culmination of the orgy, Halfjord commanded silence, saying when he could be heard: "Men of Landsvag! Harold saith he will have this our fair land. We look not kindly upon his vain boast and will take the field in person; let him who loveth Landsvag go with us, those who fear Harold remain behind."

A tremendous shout greeted this speech. Springing to their feet and brandishing drawn swords the men cried: "With thee, Halfjord!"

"I would I were a man," said Grunhilde, as with flushed cheek she watched this scene.

"Nay, sweet queen," responded Half-jord, "it pleaseth me better that thou art woman."

At this juncture, the tumult having somewhat subsided, Olaf rose and cried: "A boon, king !"

"What would Olaf ?" was the answer.

"King, thou hast a beauteous bride, fair as the day itself, but Olaf's castle is empty. When I am weary I would fain throw myself into soft arms and in the tender languishings of love forget this troublous tempest of life.   Olaf has served thee faithfully nor yet hath sued for aught thou mightest give; but now, oh, king, as sole reward for true and faithful service, I ask thy consent that Olaf wed this sweet maid even before we depart to meet the mighty Harold."   As he spoke he had gradually moved toward the girl who, remembering the afternoon scene, was shivering with fright, scarce able to sit up, yet never removing her eyes from Olaf as he drew closer until with his last words he clasped in his arms the form of the now almost unconscious Hilda.

A murmur of astonishment ran around the table. This was a most unlooked-for culmination; it might be safely said that, with the exception of Grunhilde and the two chief actors, none had dreamed that Olaf had sought the solace of love. Alric's face rivalled his hair in its fierce color, Grunhilde looked as though a serpent had stung her, Halfjord was amused, but Olga was happy, happier even than the expectant lovers, whose fate hung on one man's words.

"By Odin! Olaf, but you are hot and hasty in love as in war!" exclaimed the king, laughing, for Halfjord enjoyed the rich spice of the unexpected.

"Not so, king; this gentle heart," indicating Hilda, "was a fortress before whose sturdy walls I needs must sit in patient waiting for the space of many long and hungry hours, but now the prize is won, I ask it of my king as my rightful spoils."

Halfjord was about to speak, Grunhilde interrupted him. "Methinks," she said, "this were neither time nor place for this. See, Hilda hath not spoken, her gentle heart hath not stomach for so public an avowal as you would force upon her, Olaf. We will question her in private and according to what she saith shall Olaf's answer be.''

"Thou art right, as ever, sweet Grunhilde. We will hear this at another time, Olaf," said the king.

Olaf had intercepted a look pregnant with meaning which passed between Alric and the queen as the latter was speaking. He made no reply to the king, cast a reproachful look upon Grunhilde and returned to his seat, while Hilda raised her eyes in mute appeal to her mistress, and in response to a sign of assent from her withdrew.

The banquet, which had opened so brilliantly, was a failure ; Olaf's stern brow seemed to sit in judgment at the board, condemning the selfish gayety of the sycophants, nor were their spirits restored until both Olaf and the women retired, when the wine circulated anew, and in the excess of the cup they found intoxication's counterfeit merriment.

In the morning the king informed Olaf
that his suit had been referred entirely to
Grunhilde as the better able to pass upon
it, and shortly after he was summoned to
the queen's presence.

Grunhilde was alone; she greeted her
foster-brother with a most gracious smile.
"Ah, Olaf ! come sit you near me."

Olaf bowed without speaking, reverently
kissed the proffered hand, and took the
seat she indicated. Grunhilde silently re-
garded him for a moment, then, leaning
toward him; she asked : "Is Grunhilde less
sister now that you no longer tell her
those things which move you ? "

"Not so, sweet Grunhilde," he answered.
"I love thee still more now, for now art
thou queen as well as sister."

"And yet," she said, sadly, "time was
when Olaf would not have thought to wed
without telling Grunhilde." All the ten-
derness of the girl's nature had come to
the surface; her eyes were softly clouded
with that sweet, mysterious haze which,
rising from the depths of woman's soul, in
hiding much reveals yet more. Olaf looked,

felt guilty of he knew not what, and, tak-
ing her hand with old-time familiarity, was
about to explain to her that he had had no
opportunity of speaking, when her melting
mood vanished like the unseen flight of a
disembodied spirit.   "Methinks," she said
imperiously, "Olaf is bold   to ask the
hand of Grunhilde's maid with not a
thought of his queen."

The change in her bearing was no more
lightning-like than that in his. "Queen,"
replied he coldly, "Olaf hath asked thy
kind favor for his suit."

"When ? "

"When he asked Halfjord, queen."

"Nay, but you had bespoke the girl be-
fore even that."

"Yea, queen, Olaf's heart had so drank
of love's sweet fountain that it did over-
flow, and, thanks be to Odin, her tender
heart drank from the same stream."

The queen frowned.   "It were sport to
those who gather around our good king to
hear Olaf, whom all think wedded to the
rude art of war, or the still more dangerous
game of statecraft, sighing like a lovesick

swain over a simple maid. Verily, Olaf"
— she laughed, but there was no merriment
in the laugh — "this new fancy of yours
would give me much pleasure, save that it
must give you pain."

Olaf started from his seat — "Grun-
hilde !" he gasped.

"Yea, I speak true, Olaf. Sit you down
and hear me — hear the words of a sister,
one who loves you, Olaf, would gladly
spare you that which is to come, and yet
for her very sister's love must tell you.
Olaf, among men you are a man, but with
women you are a very child. A pretty
face has turned your thoughts in soft and
gentle strains, and you who know no guile,
think none, yet even now doth she for
whom you so hotly sigh yield to your in-
sistence, while in private she weepeth out
her bright eyes for love of another."

Woman is all heart, yet has no heart —
a paradox, you say. O yes, a paradox,
but none the less true, for the dear creature,
though that she calls her heart be full to
overflowing, will tease as the cat does the
mouse the man for whom she would give

her life ; even more—in some moods she
will wring the last drop of blood from his
heart, and, though her very soul be crushed
in the wringing, smile as she views the
wreck.

Ah ! woman ! woman !   It is well that
you know not your own power, else were
there little hope for man !   Without your
gentle presence man would find this life a
living hell, death a sweet release, and yet,
fair tempter, we are taught in holy writ
that but for you there were no such thing
as eternal hell.   Ah ! well, little maid—
creation's prize, Creator's masterpiece, we
have you, that is enough ; and though
your first act on earth was to form a part-
nership with the devil, which (pardon me)
has never yet been absolutely dissolved,
still not a man of us but would rather take
long chances on salvation *with* you than
its absolute certainty deprived of your soft
ministrations in this weary life.

Olaf, despairing, raging, half wild at
what he heard, forgot that he was in the
presence of his queen ; he gripped her
hand like a vise as he fairly shrieked :

"Grunhilde! drive me not to curse thee!
thou knowest not what thou sayest; not
even Landsvag's queen shall say to Olaf
that I have heard from thee.   Speak ; say
thou didst but play with me!"

The man's agony was terrible, but she
was cold, impassive, unyielding as stone.

"I spoke true, Olaf," she said.   He
buried his head in his hands. "Grunhilde,
I suffer!" he groaned.   Her eyes flashed.
"You suffer?   Even so do others suffer.
Is Olaf's heart to be more tenderly nur-
tured than those of less favored mor-
tals?"

There was a moment's silence; then
Olaf broke forth: "Fool that I am; I
I will not hear thee, Grunhilde, though
thou art queen, yet my heart believeth thee
not.   Hilda loves me ; nor will I doubt,
until with her own lips she telleth me she
hath lied!"

"Then from her own lips shall Olaf
hear it," was the cold response, as the
queen summoned a menial and sent for
Hilda.

The waiting was painful ; neither spoke;

Grunhilde sat wrapt in thought, Olaf went
to the casement and stood with back turned
on his queen until the sound of a soft foot-
step caused him to turn with a start and
face Hilda. The girl had evidently been
weeping ; her face was drawn and pinched.
One look only—a hungry, despairing look,
she gave Olaf when he saw not, then drop-
ped her eyes to the floor and waited as the
victim waits the executioner's axe. The
queen averted her eyes, looked first at Olaf
who had again turned to the window, then,
seeming to regard intently a distant corner
of the room, said : " Hilda, we have been
chiding Olaf for the unseemly heat with
which he spoke for your hand ; he hath
grown angry, and believeth not even his
queen that you will not wed him, where-
fore have we sent for you ; speak, that he
may hear you — will you be Olaf's bride ?"

Hilda seemed to choke, but the half-
stifled word, " No !" was heard, Olaf
thought, too plainly. Turning, he faced
the women and, with a smile of bitter irony,
said : " So ; a simple maid hath done that
no man might do — made Olaf a fool."

Suddenly his brow darkened with an angry
frown. " False as you are fair ! " he ex-
claimed, " yet not so fair as false. But a
few hours since about this neck those soft
and clinging arms entwined, the while I
drank from your too willing lips the sweet
wine of love's kiss. That tongue which
now forswears itself hath oft, forsooth,
framed tender words to thrill this rugged
heart of mine ; your face is passing fair,
your form beyond compare, your heart the
noisome resting-place of infamy and
shame." He was working himself into a
frenzy. " You a maiden?" he continued ;
" Not so ; you have a harlot's soul—I
gorge at thought of your lascivious kisses;
strange, passing strange, so fair a temple
should hold so foul a tenant. Get you
gone, girl ! my very eyes do bleed at sight
of you—get you gone ! "

Hilda was trembling like a leaf ; when
Olaf paused for want of breath her lacer-
ated woman's soul found utterance in the
gasping words, "Oh ! queen !" Grun-
hilde, apparently heedless of the girl's
torture, simply waved her hand, saying,

"Go, Hilda." She went slowly out, turning at every step to fasten her burning eyes on the man whose scorn had withered her tender heart. Like the everlastingly damned soul which, falling, falling, falling into the depths of endless perdition, yet, in agony of despair, turns ever its envious eyes upon that heaven forever lost, did she, with faltering step, with eyes that saw naught save that she left behind, pass from the paradise of love, out to the darkness of despair.

When they were again left to themselves Grunhilde spoke with some warmth: "Methinks Olaf forgetteth he speaketh in presence of his queen."

"Grunhilde," replied he, "in the presence of an outraged soul there are no earthly distinctions."

She rose and going over to him laid her hand caressingly on his shoulder. "Take it not so hard, Olaf," she said, "'tis but the lot of many men."

"Yea, and of this man, too," he answered bitterly. "Thus endeth Olaf's dream of love."

"Not so, brother, there be many women in this world."

"Ah! Grunhilde, thinkest thou that Olaf changeth like the wind from one quarter to another? Nay, in this world is none other for me."

She still clung affectionately to his arm, though at his last words she winced as though something hurt her.

"And is there no love for Olaf henceforth?" she asked.

"Nay, Grunhilde, false though she be I yet love Hilda, and none but Hilda."

"Then love none other, Olaf; love not even her for her falseness, and now that love hath gone out of your life let ambition be your stay."

She spoke with feverish intensity. Olaf was surprised. Before replying he half turned, and as he pondered, regarded her with an inquiring look. "Ambition!" said he; "That hath no meaning unto Olaf."

"Ah! Olaf! she exclaimed impetuously, "had you my ambition you would have been king of Landsvag!"

"And Halfjord?" he asked.

"Your vassal, if he lived."

Olaf did not reply at once. He was thinking ; she had suggested to him an entirely new train of thought. Finally he asked : "And Grunhilde ? "

"Your faithful servant and friend, Olaf," was her answer.

Again he paused for thought, then reached up, and taking the hand that still rested on his arm, said : "Grunhilde, learn this l Olaf hath no ambition save faithfully to serve his country and his rightful king ; Olaf hath no love save that which Grunhilde hath seen spurned." He hesitated a moment, then formally addressing her, said : "Queen, Olaf hath much to do before Landsvag goeth forth to meet Harold; I crave thy permission to depart." Her only reply was a gesture of assent.

Grunhilde, alone, stood just where he left her. At last she threw herself on the stone floor and weeping murmured : "Ah l Olaf, Olaf ! I love you not well enough to sin with you, yet too well to see another your happy bride l For me your heart is ice ; it is well l"

CHAPTER VI

Meantime, in an apartment not far remote from that Olaf had just left, another scene between lovers was enacting.

Alric, seeking Olga, had found her alone and greeting her with a kiss he asked, "Sweet Olga, what say the women of these strange events which so stir us men ?"

"What say the women? Wherefore asketh Alric such things of Olga ?" she innocently inquired.

"Olga," said Alric impatiently, "I have no time for senseless dawdling such as this; I needs must work. Have you aught to tell ?"

"Nay, why should I have ?"

"Cease this teasing !" he cried angrily. "Tell me what you hear that may advantage Alric."

The girl turned and facing him said slowly, deliberately, "Alric, for love have I

given my soul into your keeping, played
the spy upon our trusting queen and,
worming from her those secrets told only
in the quiet seclusion of the wedded cham-
ber, have brought them to your too eager
ears, inquiring not what use you make of
that I tell, yet knowing but too well you
mean no good to those who rule us.   This
have I done for love of you and what have
I in return?   Naught save the oft repeated
empty promise of him who, false to his
king, can but be false to her who too
weakly yields to his insistence.   Nay, hear
me out, Alric," she said as he sought to in-
terrupt her, "even now are you false to
Olga, but beware her vengeance !   Trai-
tress I may be, false to king, queen and
country, yet have I been true to you, Alric;
be you true to me or else I swear by the
great Odin to drag you through the dust to
shame and death ! "

Alric, startled by this sudden change of
front, sought to make light of it, asking
banteringly, "What demon possesseth
sweet Olga that she speak thus savagely ? "
at the same time seeking to embrace her.

She repulsed him as she answered, "A demón, Alric, of so frightful mien that, beholding him, mine eyes see naught save blood; my trembling hands in nervous frenzy seek to grasp the knife that floats before my gaze, a knife for your false heart, Alric. That demon is jealousy; know you his bloody countenance ? "

"Nay, sweet one, I like not such rude companions ; Alric has no doubt of Olga's love nor seeth reason why she should question his."

"Alric were fool to doubt Olga."

"Wherefore then," he asked, "doubt you Alric ? "

"They who know do say that Alric loves the maiden Hilda," was her reply.

At this he burst out laughing, "Verily, Olga, your fancies amuse me the while I chafe at this delay. Know you not that the great Olaf seeketh Hilda? Did he not even demand her of our king but a few hours since? "

"Yea, but received her not ; it is said that our queen favors Alric's suit."

" I tell you, girl, Alric hath no suit save

for you. I weary of this folly." He rose
to go but, womanlike, she detained him.

"If Alric loves not Hilda why his fierce
looks when Olaf held her in his arms ?"

"Why? Because Alric hateth Olaf, nor
can he brook happiness for him who hath
pricked Alric with his sword. Olga," he
continued savagely, "Olaf must die !"

"Nay, for Landsvag's sake must he
live."

"Not so. Is Olaf greater than Alric ?"

"Ah ! Alric, you speak to my heart
which answers 'Nay,' yet have you not told
me you love Olga."

He saw she was relenting and drawing
nearer said, " I have so often told you that
grow you not weary of hearing it?"

" Nay, Alric, I pray you grow not weary
of saying it. Once more, Alric, tell me."

" I love you, Olga," he whispered in
tones as soft as he could make them, then
added, " Now is Olga satisfied and ready to
do my bidding?"

" I am, Alric if you but tell me what
lieth before Olga, though it wounds my

heart that you are more ready to speak of your affairs than of our love."

"Then listen, girl, a throne is Olga's reward."

"A throne ? What care I for that ? I want but Alric."

"Alric will not live without a throne, hence must you have a throne to have Alric."

"Alric, I like not such words, my heart seeketh not as doth yours the false glamour of the court ; rather would I sit in quiet at your feet and hear you forever whisper sweet words of love. Besides, what throne will Alric have and where shall he get it ?"

"Leave that to me nor disturb your pretty head save to do that I say."

"Nay, Alric," she insisted, "if you love me you will tell me, nor will I do your bidding till I know."

The man hesitated He felt that he needed her, but, playing as he was a double game both in love and politics, liked not too well the thought of making of one of his victims a confidant as to the other. After pondering he concluded that any sign of distrust would make of the girl a more dangerous possibility than frank confidence; his mind was made up. "The throne of Landsvag," was what he said.

"Landsvag!" she exclaimed. "You jest, Alric."

"No, I jest not, Olga. Hear me: This Harold will win and Landsvag will be his; Halfjord and Olaf die but Alric lives."

"Yet can I not see how Alric may have this throne if Harold wins."

He lowered his voice to a whisper: "Alric will be with Harold, his reward Landsvag."

The girl stared in frozen horror at the self-confessed traitor. "Alric a traitor? Alric sell his native land? Ah! Alric, even Olga's love may hardly bear with such infamy!"

"Yes, traitor, if such it please you to call me," he answered, with an effort at a smile. "And yet" (here he essayed a softer tone), "it is for Olga's sake."

"Nay, nay, Alric, let not Olga be the cause of this foul disgrace; what care I

for crowns ?   I but wish your love, naught
in the world save that," and impulsively
she threw her arms around his neck; but
he was in no mood for tenderness beyond
what seemed necessary to keep the peace,
and disengaging himself he said:

"Leave such things to me, Olga.   Sit
you here and dream of love, if it please
your fond fancy, but keep your ears open
and let me know that which you hear;
will you do that?"

"Oh! Alric, ask me not to sell my own,
my native land!" she pleaded piteously.

"I ask naught of you, girl," he gruffly
answered, "save that you tell me what
I ask."   There was a moment's silence,
broken by Alric as he continued: "Listen,
Olga, I seek not Halfjord's ruin, but
only Alric's safety, whatever be the end.
Do that I ask and when we return Olga
shall be Alric's sweet bride—what say
you?"

Scarce half satisfied with his explana-
tion, more than delighted with his promise,
she replied: "Alric's words are as music
unto mine ears."

"And you will seek to question the queen?" he asked.

"I will, Alric," she faltered.

"Then shall Alric see you yet again before we go forth to battle."

He was about to leave her without another word, but she, springing forward, clasped her arms about him and with a voice choked with sobs begged him to tell her over and over again that he loved her. This he did with as good grace as possible and when he finally escaped his sole comment on the whole scene was a half-smothered objurgation with the mental note: "Women are fools!"

Not many hours after the scene just related Olaf, alone in his chamber, saw the curtains before the opening slightly move, then part and in the gap was framed the tear-stained, haggard, frightened face of the girl Hilda. She stood trembling, hesitating on the threshold. Olaf rudely accosted her:

"You mistake, girl; Alric's chamber lieth beyond."

The unhappy girl, recoiling as from a blow, could only gasp : "Ah! Olaf!"

"Begone, woman!" he cried. "Take your lecherous soul to him who payeth you in the hot kisses of unrighteous love. Get you gone, I say!"

"Olaf! Olaf!" she wailed, "you kill Hilda!"

"Nay," quoth he, "if so foul a thing as you did boast the frame of man my sword would drink its fill of your treacherous blood, but Olaf slayeth no woman even though that woman be a fiend."

"Your words," she said mournfully, "are sharper than your sword," then added pleadingly: "Hear me, Olaf, oh! hear me!"

"Hear you?" he echoed with a laugh of brutal harshness. "Nay, Olaf hath heard you swear love and truth, and with those selfsame lips, almost within the hour, forswear these soft and melting oaths! By Odin! Mine ears do tingle even now with sound of your perjured words; upon those lips where once did play the soft alluring smile of love now lurks the covert sneer; a woman hath accomplished that which man might never do, degraded Olaf, and you, the woman, come now with hungry heart and eager eyes to gloat over your too well accomplished task. Hear you? I have too often done that nor have I stomach for further speech with you."

He had turned his back while speaking, but when he finished she glided softly over the threshold, and laying a tremulous hand upon his arm, said, "Olaf, shame were Hilda's portion should she be discovered here."

"Yea," he replied, "that were true if so be shame might come to present degradation."

Seeming not to heed the interruption she continued, "Olaf saith Hilda hath a wanton heart, but Olaf knoweth she would not brave the ready chance of infamy save for sweet love's sake."

"Love!" he exclaimed. "You know not what love means."

"Olaf! I know but too well, seeing that I love you."

A sardonic smile was his sole reply to this · avowal, while she in feverish haste continued : "Yea, Olaf, I love you ; this much shall you hear, though you close your ears to all else which Hilda saith. I love you, Olaf, and for that love have braved the chance of shame, and even of your scorn, in coming thus to you." The girl's earnestness impressed Olaf, and though by no means convinced, he suffered her to continue without interruption. Reassured by his silence she said, " When Grunhilde questioned Hilda she spoke but one word in reply, and yet that one word tore poor Hilda's heart more than all the burning words of scornful abuse that Olaf hurled at Hilda."

Here was a suggestion most pregnant in its possibilities ; whatever Olaf's opinion of the girl's honesty it might not pass unchallenged; as yet he had given no sign of relenting, simply letting her speak, as it were, by sufferance, but her last words, seeming to tell his dead heart of the possibility of resurrection, awoke his interest. His eyes for the first time met hers ; there was no doubt that fidelity, truth, shone in those eyes, now clouded with sorrow's soft veil. He shivered, almost unconsciously he moved as if to embrace her, then catching himself, some of his old roughness came back, though his tone was less rude when he asked, "If this be so, then why did Hilda answer Grunhilde thus?"

"Why, for your sake, Olaf. Could aught else have drawn such a word from Hilda's lips?"

"For my sake? Now methinks you jest, and in most unseemly fashion. To me there seemeth no wit in such pleasantry. Leave me, woman; go while yet there is time else, being discovered, all will think of you even as doth Olaf."

Again had he grown rude and stern, but Hilda was not to be shaken off. With a woman's wit she divined that he was unaware of that which had been revealed to her, and with a woman's love she sought to tell him and in the telling save him. "Olaf," she said, "though you kill me for speaking, yet must I speak! You are in danger, and Hilda renounced your love

to save the life that unto Landsvag is
much, unto Hilda more."

Here was scent of a political plot. He
waited with every sense alert for what
should follow, but she, too, was waiting
and not until he asked, "What doth Hilda
mean?" did she unburden her heavily
charged soul.

"Olaf, after the king's banquet the
queen sent for me and told me if I loved
you I would give you up. She said there
were those in this kingdom who loved not
Olaf, yet who had too ready access to the
king's ear; that Halfjord had other plans
for you and your wedding Hilda, angering
him, would but give them the desired oppor-
tunity of poisoning the king's mind against
you. The queen, Olaf, made it your life
against Hilda's happiness; do you wonder
now that Hilda answered 'No' to the ques-
tion if she would wed you? Olaf, you
have doubted Hilda, and in your rude
anger have even cursed her with words
that did shrivel her very soul, whose fire
hath all but dried up the fountains of her
tears. Yet, oh! Olaf, my heart hath ever

been true to you since first mine ears heard your sweet words of love. I love you, Olaf, nor may other than Olaf ever call Hilda his, and yet for that very love have I refused the sweet joy of lying in your loving arms."

Olaf heard what she had to say, first with incredulity, next with momentarily increasing anger. Hilda paused, waiting for some answer, but he spoke not; his face distorted with frightful passion, he stood seeming unconscious of her presence; her hand dropped from his arm. Moving a pace or two from him she looked closely at him, then, extending her arms, she uttered in a tone of appeal, almost a wail, the one word, "Olaf!"

He raised his head, and, fixing upon the girl a searching gaze, asked: "Will Hilda swear to the truth of that she saith?"

"Yea, Olaf, I swear," was the earnest reply.

Advancing, he took her in his arms, saying as he did so: "It seemeth to me those eyes are windows of a soul that knows no guile; I do believe you, sweet Hilda," add-

ing, as he looked fondly at her now radiant
face, "Had you not veiled those sweet
eyes when you did speak in answer to
Grunhilde's question, I should then have
seen that the word which turned my soul
into a seething pit of demonlike fury came
not from your heart."

Whispering soft nothings in her willing
ears, Olaf was, for a time, lost to all but the
sweet sense of renewed love ; but, with re-
turning consciousness of the present, his
eye kindled and a harsher note rang in
his voice as he asked : "So Grunhilde told
you this ? "

"Yea, Olaf."

"What meant she by such lies ?" was
his almost unconscious query.

"Lies, Olaf ?" innocently inquired the
girl.

"Yes, Hilda, lies. Lies forged for the
single purpose of killing this, our love ;
lies spoken to you in hope your simple
heart would too readily believe them ; lies
she dared not utter before Olaf, who would
laugh even his queen to scorn did she seek
to tell him such things."

"Nay, nay, Olaf," protested Hilda; "surely you do wrong our good queen."

Smiling sarcastically, he said: "Olaf had but just returned when Hilda said that Grunhilde did love Olaf; hath Olaf been less kind to Grunhilde than Hilda? I say she lies, and find good proof of that I say. You say she is forsworn unto her own liege lord. Which were the harsher charge, good Hilda?

"Chide me not, Olaf: I spoke in silly fear," she said, blushing, meanwhile; "but it was love bespoke the fear when I did say Grunhilde loved you."

"Then you think Grunhilde loveth not Olaf?"

"Nay, Olaf, nor yet that she hath lied to me. She is too pure to love one and wed another; too good to give unnecessary pain; that which she said may be false, yet do I believe she thought it true."

"There are you wrong, then, maiden," said he, sternly. "Grunhilde is false."

"Olaf, Olaf, have a care what you say!" she cried in affright.

"Nay, Hilda, hear me out. Grunhilde

lieth when she telleth you that aught of danger to Olaf lieth in our love. This she telleth you, knowing you have no care nor thought for the dark ways of politics, and in your innocence blindly believe all that is told you. When first you spoke of Grunhilde's love for me I laughed the thought to scorn, but now, by Odin! I half believe this silly fancy, since it giveth ready clue to her most cruel lies to you."

Olaf was growing angry again. Raising his hand aloft he exclaimed : "Grunhilde, as a sister did I protect and nourish thee ; as a queen will I lay down my life for thee, but beware how thou triflest with the happiness of her who hath won Olaf's heart. For every tear thou causeth her to shed shall floods of brine pour from your eyes ; where she weepeth for a lost love shalt thou in ceaseless grief bemoan thy lost kingdom, false queen."

Hilda, terror-stricken, sought in vain to silence him. "Olaf," she gasped, "if any should hear you your words were treason."

"Treason ? If so be, then let it be. Olaf is no traitor, but Olaf brooketh not

that which causeth you to weep—nay, not
even for Landsvag." After a brief pause,
he spoke with more composure. "Hear
me, Hilda; when Olaf returneth from
teaching this Harold that Landsvag may
not be lightly assailed, then shall you be
Olaf's bride, nor shall Halfjord dare refuse
me, even though his fair queen shall storm
and rave. Before Olaf in weak submission
standeth by and seeth sweet Hilda's eyes
aswim with tears drawn from her bleeding
heart, Olaf will himself destroy the throne
he made, hurl king and queen from their
too lofty seats, and bury beneath the frag-
ments of their throne the false Grunhilde,
the weak and yielding Halfjord. Be you
ready, maiden, for my return ; meantime
hold your peace."

"Your return ? Ah ! Olaf, I fear me you
will not return. My heart sinketh with
terror at thought of this rude combat you
seek."

"Never fear, girl, we shall yet be united.
Go you now, sweet Hilda, lest being seen
your fair name should suffer."

"I shall see you, Olaf, before you go ?"

"Yea, a parting kiss from those sweet
lips shall be both my talisman and my guer-
don," was his gallant reply as she slipped
out and sped silently down the long pas-
sageway, he straining his eyes for the last
glimpse of her fleeting figure.

Olaf's mind was made up. He would
free Landsvag from Harold's clutches and
then demand Hilda, wed her in the face of
opposition and if necessary unseat his un-
grateful monarch. Having decided on his
course he made no reference whatever to
the subject when, a short time after his in-
terview with Hilda, he saw the king. Half-
jord, deeming this silence evidence of sat-
isfaction, felicitated himself upon so ready
a settlement of a question which, in view
of the queen's determined opposition, had
bid fair to become embarrassing.

The troops were already gathering, the
plain stretching beneath the castle pre-
sented a stirring sight filled as it was with
moving bodies of hardy warriors, their
arms flashing in the sunlight while their
rude merriment, fierce oaths and war-cries
reached even the chamber where the king

and Olaf stood watching them.   The min-
ister was thoughtful, the king confident,
elated.   "See! Olaf," exclaimed the lat-
ter.   "A most goodly array; let Harold
look to himself when such as these are let
loose at him!"

"Yea, king," Olaf answered pensively.
"A brave body of valiant warriors, yet I
would they sought any other foe than Har-
old."   Something in the distance caught
his eye—a solitary horseman speeding
over the level plain; pointing to him he
said: "Methinks yon rider hath the look
of Alric; whither goeth he alone?"

Though the question was really ad-
dressed to none the king answered it, "To
join Jorg and see that our defences are
ready before our coming.   Svend leadeth
Alric's men till we come up with him."

Olaf frowned.   "King," he said, "Jorg
needeth none to watch him, surely not one
such as Alric.   Thou hast done wrong not
to keep Alric with thee—he hath a trai-
tor's heart though thou callest him friend."

"By Odin! Olaf," exclaimed the king
angrily, "methinks you have naught but

unkind words for any whom Halfjord call-
eth friend!"

Olaf's sole reply to this was a reproach-
ful glance before which Halfjord's eye fell,
and after a short discussion covering the
final arrangements for the march they sep-
arated, nor did they again meet until they
were mounted and ready for the field.

Halfjord had readily consented when
Alric asked that he be allowed to ride ahead
for the purpose of coöperating with old
Jorg, and Alric no sooner secured the de-
sired permission than he prepared for the
journey.

When all was ready he craved and was
granted an audience with the queen.
Grunhilde was alone when Alric entered
and saluting her he said, "Fair queen, I
ride in advance of our army that when we
arrive before this boasting Harold of the
south naught may be lacking."

"You do well, Alric; may Odin give
you a fair ride and a true sword."

Dropping on one knee before her he
drew his sword, and presenting it to her
said: "Will Landsvag's queen deign to

touch with her lips this sword that, being consecrated to her service, it may be invincible ? "

Grunhilde smilingly took the sword, and kissing the blade returned it saying : " Let no foe lower the sword which Grunhilde's lips have pressed."

Alric rose as he received his sword back, hesitated a moment, then said : " Queen, I go to face the foes of this land ; before I leave I fain would ask of thee a vow."

"What would you, Alric ? " she inquired, seeing that he waited encouragement.

"The queen's promise that on my return Hilda shall be mine."

"That have you, Alric ; go, when you return myself will give unto your keeping the gentle maid for whom you so lustily sigh."

" I am content.   There remaineth now naught for Alric to do save in the very front of battle to wield this sword which thou hast blessed. Queen, give Alric a battle-cry."

"Let it be ' Death to Foes ! ' "

"'Death to Foes!' be it — a cry from my queen's lips!"

"A valiant man," murmured the queen as he left her. "Ah! I would I were a man to handle so sharp a toy as Alric's blade, to drive the foe as doth our doughty Olaf!"

As Alric passed rapidly from his interview with the queen he suddenly came face to face with Olga. "Sweet Olga," he exclaimed, "give Alric one kiss that he may confound his foes, and returning crown his life with the benediction of your love. Have you aught to tell before I go?" Then seeing that she made no reply, he looked for the first time closely at her, recoiling as he did so before the stern judgment written in every line of her face. Alric was both brave and ready-witted, but found himself now at a loss to account for this sudden change, hence at a loss to know how to act.

"Doth Alric's leaving so distress fair Olga?" he asked tenderly.

The girl laughed harshly. "Go, Alric, go," she said. "Be as false to Harold as

you have been to Olga and you will be
true to Landsvag ; but come not back
seeking for your bride Hilda." She moved
past him as she spoke, and turning but to
hiss the word "Traitor!" disappeared,
leaving Alric dumbfounded and not a lit-
tle disturbed. But that worthy individual
soon regained his *sang froid*, and, mutter-
ing his favorite sentence, "Women are
fools!" betook himself to his waiting
horse, just as Olaf had entered the king's
apartments, and, when Olaf looked out on
the scene below, Alric was galloping like
the mad across the country.

CHAPTER VII

Alric rode rapidly with the air of a man burdened with a great mission; neither rider nor horse were allowed much rest as he pressed on to the front. Halfjord, had he seen him, would have commended his zeal; Olaf, wondering, would have still doubted.

It is not necessary for us to follow Alric on his long and lonely ride; suffice it to say that on reaching the territory governed by Jorg he made a wide detour and, avoiding the castle as well as any roving bands of watchers, bore his way steadily to the frontier.

The same night that Alric crossed Landsvag's boundary Harold, who had at last struck camp and was now at the foot of those rugged hills that frowningly separated him from the land of Olaf and Halfjord — Harold, waiting for the sun that he

might begin anew the march, was issu-
ing final instructions when an officer ap-
proached and announced that a man from
Landsvag would speak with him.   Har-
old's face brightened.   "Ah! hath our
good Olaf again sought us?" he ex-
claimed.

"Nay, king," said the man, "this is not
Olaf."

"Who then is he, Magnus?"

"His name, king, know I not, but he
hath a strange and savage aspect; even in
the night his hair seemeth to be of fire or
mayhap of blood, and so foul a presence
hath he that had I not touched him with
these arms I should fear me he was one of
those demons who ever seek to do evil
unto man."

Harold was a grade above the supersti-
tions of his time — that is, while believing
them, he dared to brave them, this fear-
lessness being in large measure the basis
of his hold upon his men since they, see-
ing him pass unscathed through many
tests, naturally believed that he was in
league with their gods.   "Let him be

brought hither," was the king's animated reply to Magnus, who, bowing, departed, while the king addressed those around him : " Ye shall see this demon whom Magnus bringeth unto us."

When Alric was presented not even Harold was able to conceal a slight shudder, while Eric whispered to Hengis, " Verily, Magnus saith true ; this man hath much the look of an evil one."

" What seek you ? " asked the king as Alric saluted the entire group.

" Harold whom they call 'The Fairhaired ;' he it is I seek," was the reply.

" Whence come you ? "

" From Landsvag."

" They who dwell there are Harold's enemies ; why seek you him ? "

" It were better, king, thou didst hear the man from Landsvag before thou callest him a foe," responded Alric.

" Why call you me 'king ?' "

" It needeth not an eye so quick as Alric's to see that thou art every inch a king without taking note of thy hair, which hath the sheen of gold."

"You have a sharp eye and a ready tongue. Yea, I am king, what would you with me?"

"A word in thine ear, king."

Harold, doubting the sincerity of the man, hesitated in placing himself virtually at his mercy. "You ask a strange favor," he said. "A warring king granteth not unto those against whom he wars a private audience."

"Yet didst thou give this favor unto Olaf, though he brought naught save boastful words—Alric bringeth sure means of victory and peace."

"Perchance the peace of the grave," muttered Eric.

Alric heard and, glancing at the speaker, said: "If thou doubtest me, king, let him who even now hath spoken, remain, the rest retire."

Harold consenting to this the three were soon left alone when the king asked: "What would you with Harold? Speak."

"King," said the man, "I come to offer thee Landsvag."

"What!" exclaimed Harold in surprise. "Hath Halfjord then accepted our terms ?"

"Nay, king, even now is Halfjord on the road with a mighty host to dispute thy way."

"How, then, say you that you come to offer Harold that which he seeketh ?"

"King, Halfjord would keep but Alric will deliver thee this Landsvag."

Harold made but little effort to conceal his contempt of the self-avowed traitor when he asked : "How will Alric do that he sayeth ?"

"King, I do command the left wing of the army, which shall meet thee—at the proper time Alric joineth his force with thine—thou canst see the result."

"Yea, the ruin of a brave army through the treachery of one of its own leaders. Alric, Harold would win by fairer means, nor love I the sound of your words, yet may I not lightly refuse this chance which giveth with loss of fewer men that which I wish. What doth Alric wish ? for surely he turneth not his back upon his friends without hope of reward."

"That were easily answered, king — naught save the governorship of Landsvag and fair Hilda for my bride."

" Who is Hilda ? "

" Maid to the Queen Grunhilde, king."

" Enough, Hilda shall be yours."

"And Landsvag, Harold ? "

"Also, if so you live."

Alric's eyes glistened ; throne and bride were won at the same throw. " I shall live, king !" he exclaimed.

"Not if the sword of Harold cometh near you," muttered the king to himself, as, turning the man over to Eric, he left the spot.

Eric was delighted ; himself half a traitor he found congeniality in this knave, who would sell his birthright for a mess of pottage. These two worthies spent an hour or more in close communion, parting only when Alric deemed it prudent that he should return, fearing to betray his plans by too great delay in reaching Jorg.

After parting with Alric Eric made his way at once to Harold, who greeted him with: "Hath that bastard of Landsvag gone?"

"Yea, king, to fulfill his promise."

"Promise? Ah! yes, foul fiend that he is, I would I had spurned him and trusted but to this my good sword, these my valiant men. I have no love for traitors who suck the blood of those who feed them. It were a kingly act to apprise Halfjord of this Alric's plot, that he may strangle him and squeeze out his poisonous life. Then when we meet, man to man, let the glory belong to him who earneth it by the might of his arm, not by robbery. By Thor! I will do it, though it cost me my kingdom! Seek me, Eric, a trusty messenger."

Eric returned shortly with a man, of whom he said: "King, Saggi will do thy bidding, though he die."

"It is well," said the king. "Mount the fleetest horse in the camp, ride to Halfjord and tell him Harold seeketh to conquer but by force of arms or honorable capitulation. Tell him the leader of his left wing, Alric, who hath a head even like his

treacherous blood, seeketh to betray him.
Ride, Saggi, and seek no rest till you have
found Halfjord ; an hundred pounds of
silver if you do safe deliver this message.
By all the gods of our race, Eric ! Harold
spurneth this dastard plot, which seeketh
to steal a triumph that our arms are yet
strong enough to win ! Begone, Saggi."
The man, saluting, left at once, Eric with
him, but Halfjord never recéived the mes-
sage, nor was the messenger ever again seen.

Early the next morning Alric presented
himself at Jorg's castle, with the news that
Halfjord was already on his way to meet
the invaders. The old warrior, though
liking not the seeming lack of confidence
implied by Alric's ostensible mission, and
still less pleased with the agent chosen by
the king, was too loyal to allow personal
umbrage to interfere with the duty before
him. Alric, zealous, watchful, sought in
every way to aid, and so earnest was he in
his work, so aggressive in the frequent
skirmishes now that Harold had crossed
the border, that Jorg began to trust him,
to fear he had misjudged him, and when

Halfjord finally arrived the old man took the first favorable opportunity of telling Olaf how well Alric had acquitted himself.

After the departure of Halfjord's army, which left for the front the day after Alric rode away, the great castle of the king seemed deserted. Grunhilde, who had chosen to ride some distance with her lord, turning back only when he insisted, and even then watching with longing eyes the brave cavalcade as it swept grandly across the broken plain toward the hills, whose soft blue outlines were scarce discernible in the distance; Grunhilde, with her thoughts on the field, her heart rebellious over the restrictions of her sex, found life in the castle very dull, and after a few days sought the change of a visit to her childhood's home, where she and Olaf had spent together so many sweet and happy hours in peace and innocence. She took of her ladies Hilda and Olga alone, seeming to seek solitude and quiet rather than diversion, though her expressed reason for the change was the dreariness of the royal castle.

Since her last interview with Olaf Hilda had been distrait, lost, as it were, in troubled dreams, starting guiltily when spoken to; the sad resignation following that conference with the queen in which she had renounced Olaf had given place to this frightened restlessness, the semi-consciousness of a dream, but Grunhilde gave no sign of noticing the change.

However heedless of Hilda's distress Grunhilde was quick to detect evidence of Olga's disturbed mind, as the girl had changed almost in a moment from a merry, rollicking maiden, whose wit often enlivened tedious hours, to a woman upon whose shoulders seemed to rest the weight of the universe; dreading to be alone, yet shunning company, never speaking now save when addressed, and then in few words, in tones full of unshed tears; at times with staring eyes, seeming to gaze upon frightful phantoms hovering in the air, forgetful of her lightest duties, sobbing when reminded of them, she was not even a memory of her former self. On the day that the troops left, Grunhilde, who was really quite fond of both of these girls, had kindly asked her the trouble which seemed to have overwhelmed her so suddenly, but the question had brought forth such a torrent of tears she refrained from pressing it.

These maids might be allowed to mope when others were around, but now that they were her sole companions, save the menials who came and went, it was asking too much to expect the queen to be longer patient. The cause of Hilda's sorrow Grunhilde knew only too well, nor did she have the heart to chide her for grieving over the iron that she herself had driven into the poor girl's soul, but she might reprove her by indirection, as it were, and so choosing a time when the two were with her she began on Olga, casting from time to time meaning glances at the trembling Hilda.

"Olga," she said, "we would have your thoughts with us, and, though you sigh at absence of your plighted swain who now draweth sword in defense of Landsvag, yet might you smile before your queen. *You* have but a lover in the field, *Grunhilde* both husband, king and kingdom, yet Grunhilde sigheth not save at this dullness. Weep if you will, but weep alone ; I would have my merry Olga back."

Twice Olga essayed to speak and, choking, stopped. At last she murmured faintly : "Ah ! queen, thy merry Olga returneth never."

" Are you fool, girl ? Your lover returneth, or if it be so he return not, yet will he find a glorious death. Be not so heavy of heart ; let your thoughts for a time run on pleasanter themes. Come, smile, Olga, smile."

" Nay, queen, the lips smile not save when the heart laugheth with glee. Oh ! queen, my heart is over-heavy, yet not with truant thoughts of absent lover — Olga hath no lover."

" If it be not love, then what may so bruise a maiden's heart ? Your queen, Olga, hath much love for you, nor doth it please her that your sweet face wears such dark frowns."

The girl's lips quivered, tears slowly trickled down her cheeks. Hilda, for the nonce forgetful of her own sorrow, looked on compassionately. Grunhilde was deeply touched by the girl's suffering, for Grunhilde had a warm woman's heart, a heart that knew no cruelty save when ambition jarred its sweet strings or love denied, sang in soft nocturnes another's joy, her sorrow. Full of that melting kindness which, in minor chord, sings its sweet song through woman's softened tones, the queen reached over and, laying upon Olga's head a hand in whose every fibre tingled the electric sympathy of sex, said kindly: "Olga, what driveth the smile from your lips and bringeth into your eyes these hot tears that do heat themselves in the raging fires of your tempestuous soul?"

Olga broke down completely. "Queen, have mercy on me! have mercy on me! I have sinned!" she wailed between convulsive sobs.

"Sinned? What mean you, Olga?" asked the astonished queen, to whom the whole scene was an enigma.

"Oh! queen! my heavy thoughts are with none who draw the sword for Landsvag, but with Landsvag itself."

"Verily, Olga, you do speak strange words which have no meaning to mine ears; speak, girl, and have done with mystery."

The unhappy maiden threw herself on her face before Grunhilde and almost shrieked : "Pardon! pardon, oh! queen, before I speak, else I fear I find not voice for that I would say!"

"It is granted, Olga; methinks your sin cannot be as grievous as you would make it."

"Hear, then, oh! queen," said Olga, groveling in the dust before her mistress. "Treason reareth its bloody head in Half-jord's army."

"Treason!" exclaimed the now thoroughly aroused queen.

"Yea, Grunhilde, foul treason. Alric of the bloody head would sell Landsvag unto Harold."

"Alric a traitor? Why told you not this before, miserable creature? Is Olga privy to this pretty plot?"

"Ah! queen, spare me, I implore thee; my heart upbraideth me enough without the sting of thy sharp words! Listen, queen: Olga loved Alric, even so did Alric say he loved Olga, but Alric was false. When I did think him true I played the spy upon thee, bearing unto him all that thou didst do and say; then it was he told me of his evil intent, but then I thought he loved me and, queen, though it be treason, then would I rather Landsvag had been lost than Alric. But the day when Alric set out to make his bloody bargain, Olga, even when spying upon thee, did hear him ask of thee the hand of this maid, Hilda, whom thou didst promise, and then did I know he was as false to me as to Landsvag."

Grunhilde could brook almost anything but that which jeopardized her crown. Springing up she grasped the terrified woman by the hair as she hissed: "Traitress! Why made you not this known before the knave escaped?"

"Ah! queen, I feared," gasped the girl; " my heart commanded but my tongue refused its office and the weight of Alric's crime has rested on my soul."

"Wretched woman! Even now hath Halfjord doubtless met with Harold and if that you say be true then is Landsvag lost for your too slothful speech. Hear me, if Alric betrayeth Halfjord you die!"

Olga heard not the last words—merciful nature coming to her rescue, she had swooned and lay an inert mass before the enraged queen. Hilda, who had been an amazed spectator of this tragedy, timidly approached Grunhilde.

"Queen," she said, "mayhap there yet remaineth time to warn Halfjord."

"How, girl? There be none here I may trust with such message unto him unless perchance you should take the form of man and on the wings of the wind ride you to his camp."

"I would I were a man, queen," was the gentle Hilda's reply, met with a harsh laugh as her mistress said :

"Were you a man, Hilda, the very birds would flap their wings in your face, nor betake themselves to flight when you should draw your gleaming blade. Call hither our men, Hilda, that they may remove this false and perjured wench ; her fate doth hang upon what news there cometh from Halfjord."

Hilda hesitated a moment, her heart full of gentle sympathy, but a glance at the queen's stern face showed her this was no time to intercede and, summoning the men, she silently watched them lift and bear away the inanimate form of her companion. The people had scarcely left with their burden when the queen dismissed Hilda, who retired to her apartment; Hilda's chamber looked to the east, where Olaf now was, and for hours she sat looking vacantly toward the eastern horizon. Perhaps Olaf was in danger ; nay, surely he was if danger had assailed Landsvag, for Olaf and Landsvag were one. Oh! if she had but the wings of a bird how swiftly she would fly to him; could she but save him and with him the land he so dearly loved she could die content.

Night had set in before Hilda, rousing, summoned Arne, an old woman formerly

her nurse, one whom she could trust im-
plicitly. "Arne," she said, when the woman
appeared, "I have need of you. Can you
get me a fleet horse, one which tireth
not?"

"Yea, Hilda," answered the old woman;
"but what need have you of a horse at this
hour?"

"Ask me naught, Arne, but do my bid-
ding." The woman, grumbling a little,
went out, returning shortly to announce
that the steed was ready. "Now help me,
Arne," and Hilda began hastily to prepare
herself for a journey. The woman obeyed
with a poor grace. It was evident she did
not approve of the hidden project, proba-
bly because it *was* hidden.

"Now, Arne," said Hilda, when she was
equipped to her satisfaction, "I go on a
long journey. On the morrow, should the
queen ask for me, you have but to say to
her that I go to deliver her message — she
will understand."

"Mayhap," grunted the old woman;
"but Arne understandeth not; I have no
love for a maiden's night rides."

"Peace, Arne, and do as I bid you. Now lead the way. Nay, stay ; I charge you to deliver this message unto the queen — nay, more, I would have you swear to give it her."

"What shall I swear, seeing that I know not the message ?"

"Say unto her that Hilda hath great hope that naught may befall Olga. Swear that you will do my will."

"Yea, I swear, though it seemeth unto me a silly speech and a sillier oath. Why should aught befall Olga ?"

" Peace, Arne. Do you as I have told you, and leave the rest to me. Now, I go — lead the way."

At midnight the queen, turning drowsily on her couch, heard a confused murmur, the clatter of hoofs in the courtyard, then all was silent and she fell asleep, dreamily uttering the one word, " Olaf," as a horse, urged on by its strange rider, dashed through the sombre night toward the home of the rising sun.

CHAPTER VIII

Harold's inactivity was the occasion of much surprise to both Halfjord and Olaf, and various were the conjectures by which they sought to account for the unusual quiet which, according to Jorg's regular reports, reigned on the border.

"Methinks this mighty Harold feareth Landsvag," was the king's comment on one occasion, to which Olaf, who, himself of heroic mold, had, or thought he had, divined the nature of his foe, replied : " King, it seemeth unto me that Harold waiteth for us that he may take no undue advantage."

"But that were not, Olaf, the deed of a great general."

"True, king, it were not war; but methinks it were like Harold."

"This Harold seemeth to have enchanted you," was the king's almost angry response.

"Halfjord," said Olaf, "if seeing a noble

soul and doing it homage, if wishing that one who is great were your brother rather than your enemy, be enchantment, then hath Harold enchanted Olaf; yet shall I seek to cut his throat when we shall meet; yea, with all my strength seek to slay him, and then, when it is done, sit me down and grieve over the noble life which hath taken flight through the gaping rent my own true weapon shall make."

"I warrant you will fight valiantly, Olaf, but it seemeth unto me you have for this Harold a feeling most akin to love."

Olaf pondered for a moment, then answered so seriously that Halfjord could not mistake his sincerity: "King, I *do* love Harold."

This honest reply nettled Halfjord. "And your own king?" he asked hotly.

"Knoweth that he hath Olaf's heart and faith, nor feareth aught from this selfsame love of a generous foe."

The question had no sooner been asked than the king's own generosity of soul reproved him, himself a man whose soul, dwarfed in its greatness by the weakness of the physical man, was yet capable of grand deeds. He felt the instinctive reverence inspired by the virtuous in the hearts both of truth and vice, and, mollified, answered at once : "Yea, Olaf, Halfjord feareth naught from you."

Still, despite his words, Olaf's evident admiration for Harold disturbed the king, since it suggested the thought that Olaf, though everlastingly true to his present king, would have been better pleased had he been born to follow the fortunes of Harold. Perhaps Halfjord's half-formed conviction was correct.

Human nature is strangely complex, and human judgment, corrupted by the contamination of its fleshly tabernacle, strangely deficient. The great army of unmarked heroes is lost to our sight the while we offer the incense of praise before the shrines of the favored few; the shadow of a mouse obscures a mountain. Ridiculous? Yes, ridiculous, and yet, in good sooth, it does. Were the three hundred at Thermopylæ less valiant than Leonidas? You answer "No." Yet history gives but the one

name. Had Cambronne a more gigantic
soul than each one of that remnant of the
Old Guard which, unconquerable, held the
field of Waterloo after the star of France
had set ? Again you say " No." Yet name
me even one of them. You cannot. It is
ever so. How many Miltons have gone
down to the cheerless grave, bearing in
their overcharged souls deathless songs
which, let us hope, a more generous world
beyond will hear ? Yon street gamin may,
with fair chance, distance in the race of
life the man who now grudgingly buys his
paper.

The hackneyed phrase of greatness a
birthright, greatness won and compulsory
greatness is on every tongue, but what of
opportunity — yes, what of opportunity ?
Man is judged chiefly by his successes — a
brutal, barbaric basis for damnation or ele-
vation.

In climbing the Alps of Switzerland,
men go bound with one common rope for
common protection. One slips, the rest,
bracing themselves, support the fallen one
until, regaining his feet, he moves once

more upward to the crowning summit that pierces the sky above him.   But in climbing the treacherous, glacier-covered, moraine-broken, crevasse-pierced Alps of life how is it, brother?   Seek not to tie yourself to my rope — I have all that I can do to drag myself up — and if you get above me and, with eyes fixed on the towering crest above, in your eagerness slip and fall, I, coming up with you, have no helping hand to lend you.   No, no, I will give you ever so gentle a kick, sending you bounding back down the steep slope, and, in my self-satisfaction will call lustily to those around and below me to do the same. Each foot spurns the quivering mass until, at last, the bleeding, bruised and mangled soul lands in the only resting-place — hell — which opens its greedy jaws to receive the morsel we have thrown it.

Sometimes one who is not entirely dead to sympathy heeds the cry of the weaker soul, essays the task of lifting his brother, but woe to him if he whom he succors should fall, dragging him down in the fall, for in such a case but one word knows this world: "Fool!" and that fool the man who put a double strain upon the rope that anchored his own soul.

Your pardon, good reader, for this digression (which, by the way, you will probably skip as of no personal interest to you). Of course *you* would not refuse a helping hand, but then your neighbor would and are you not just a bit grateful to me for exposing to you his meanness? Now this entire homily means but one thing—that Olaf was as great a man as Harold, but the world knows nothing to-day of Olaf because Harold was victor.

Early in the morning of the third day's march a messenger from Jorg arrived bringing news that Harold had crossed the boundary, and that on the day he left Alric had repulsed the advance guard of the invaders. Halfjord was delighted.

"See, Olaf!" he exclaimed, "Alric with his few horsemen hath discomfited their vanguard; verily, they will melt like the snow beneath the sun when this our mighty array confronteth them."

Olaf knew better, but contented himself with shaking his head silently and, dropping behind he beckoned to Jorg's courier, questioning him closely as they rode, but the man could give him no information on the subject he most wished to know—regarding Alric—as the fellow left shortly after Alric's arrival and knew nothing save that he was there and had led the troops in the skirmish.

As they drew near the border, about a day's ride from Jorg's castle, Halfjord and Olaf left the army and rode ahead, discussing as they rode the plans for the impending battle. Olaf was filled with dismay when he learned that the command of the left wing, which he proposed to give Erling, had already been promised Alric.

"Halfjord!" he cried warningly, "thou dost rush blindly into thine own snare; beware, king, beware; it were better that Alric and all his men should leave us than that he should lead that day. I tell thee the man hath a traitor's heart and will sell thee and thy land for a bauble!"

Fate had decreed that Alric should betray his king and fate shut the king's eyes, closed his ears. What Olaf said only served to make him indignant and, after a hot dispute in which the king bitterly reproached Olaf for his enmity to his (the king's) favorites, the young man made no further reference to the subject, nor did Alric's name again pass his lips except when speaking to Jorg and Erling, just before the battle, he said : "Let your eyes be ever upon Alric and slay him if he seems to be either traitorous or luke-warm."

The king and Olaf when they entered Jorg's castle were received with acclamations and found the men in high spirits over their recent successes. No time was lost in getting to the front. Halfjord put himself at the head of the troops in the castle and, the morning after his arrival, started with them toward the distant plain where Harold's busy camp could but just be discerned. Olaf, with a small escort of picked men, rode some distance in advance and, coming suddenly upon a roving band of foragers, he routed them, capturing one whom he released with the injunction, "Go tell Harold Olaf is here."

Halting a few miles from the enemy's camp Halfjord now waited the arrival of his main army. This came up during the night, and in the early morning Harold saw deploy into position before him the legions of his doughty foe. He watched them with interest, commenting freely on their soldierly appearance and gallant bearing; but let it not be thought that while he watched them he was himself idle; his own troops were taking position at the same time, and now were facing each other two mighty, composite engines of destruction—waiting but a word for the beginning of their dreadful work.

As the two lines of sentient clay stood watching with hungry eyes each the other, Harold rode alone slowly to the front and, reaching a point about midway between the opposing forces, drew rein and, raising his hand, waved it toward Halfjord's line, at the same time calling, "Olaf! Olaf!"

The young man, who had been closely watching this move, heard his name called and rode forward rapidly to meet, as he thought, his challenger, but when he drew near Harold said : "Olaf, I love you ; you are a man ; it pleaseth me not to think I shall kill you, yet so shall it be. I fain would clasp in friendliness your sword-hand before we seek to kill."

Olaf's manly heart was deeply touched. "Verily," he said, "thou hast a lofty soul, great Harold. I love thee even as thou sayest thou dost love Olaf, but I shall kill thee though thy death will greatly grieve me. My heart leapeth at chance of once more in honorable friendship taking thy hand—here is mine!" And now was witnessed the most remarkable sight that ever yet was seen — there, before two vast armies eager to get at one another's throats, the leaders of these hosts—one a king, the other kingly—two grand souls instinctively rendering homage unto one another—paid graceful tribute each to the other, sealing a compact of friendship to be broken in one short hour by the death of one at the other's hand. Raising aloft their left hands they clasped with iron grip

the hand of fellowship. Not a word more
was spoken ; silently, almost mournfully,
they gazed into one another's eyes, then,
releasing their grasp, turned and, before
the astonished gaze of the assembled thou-
sands, rode slowly back to their respective
posts.

At the very moment that Harold and
Olaf clasped hands a haggard, breathless
woman dashed into the court-yard of ·
Jorg's castle, leaping from the saddle just
as her noble steed sank lifeless to the
ground. A hurried question, an answer,
and, without pausing for rest or refresh-
ment, securing a new mount, the strange
woman swept out and was soon seen rid-
ing in a mad gallop in the wake of Half-
jord's army.

The armies were marshalled in a com-
paratively narrow valley ; behind Halfjord
were broken, ragged hills, in Harold's
rear a stream fordable in but few places.
The invader had no advantage in position;
defeat meant to him destruction, and still,
though his generals muttered words of angry
doubt, he with strange prescience fore-

saw the inevitable result and, *guadium certaminis*, the victor's aureole upon his brow, calmly awaited the arrival of destiny.

The left wing of Halfjord's army under Alric was brought by the encroaching hills quite near to Harold's right, where Eric led. Thus Nature herself seemed to favor the conspirators against the integrity of Landsvag. Olaf commanded the center, directly opposite Harold, who personally led his men ; Jorg had charge of Landsvag's extreme right ; Erling, at Olaf's request, had placed his men at the left of the center and sought to keep a watchful eye on Alric as well as on the field ; the king himself, while assuming general charge of operations, was too eager for the combat to tie himself to any one part of the line and had stationed himself, with some two hundred of his most valiant warriors, a short distance in front of the main column, intending at the signal to hurl himself against the compact line, a living wedge driven by that mighty force behind, hoping also to engage Harold in personal combat.

The last friendly word spoken Harold
and Olaf had returned to their lines; the
two great columns stood for a brief mo-
ment quivering with excitement, and dur-
ing the respite Alric galloped over to
where Svend, rigid as a rock, sat his horse;
neither spoke as the rider neared his im-
perturbable lieutenant; a glance of inquiry
from one, of assurance from the other,
was sufficient; Alric's mind was easy, if
the mind of a traitor may ever be easy, and
he rode back to his station and prepared
for the charge.

The trumpets sounded, and with a
mighty shout that seemed to split the very
heavens the living masses swept forward,
looking as they rushed over the undulating
ground like the unwinding coils of two
Titan serpents. Like the sweeping rush of
the wind-swept storm Halfjord and his
picked band, a mere warning of that be-
hind, threw themselves against the wall
that now advanced to meet them. Lands-
vag's king was easily distinguished. Har-
old divined his purpose as to himself, but
his word was given to Olaf, and muttering,

"When I have done with Olaf, Halfjord," he rode along his line beyond the reach of the first shock, then, turning, galloped across the field to a point where he anticipated the rapidly advancing Olaf would meet him.

The first fortunes of the day were clearly with Landsvag. Halfjord, cutting his way through quivering flesh, had opened the way for those who followed in his wake, and, turning to ride back, his men mingled with Olaf's rushing through the breach. Jorg, old war-dog that he was, at the first onset rolled Harold's left up like a scroll, and already a part of his force was between Harold and the river, while on the left Alric was pressing the enemy hard. Such was the situation when Olaf met Harold and cried: "Yield thee, Harold! Yield while yet there is time! See! Thy men fly like birds before the storm; the day is ours. Yield thee, king!"

Harold only smiled, though to the onlooker disaster seemed about to overwhelm him. "Olaf," he said, "for defeat look to your own men. As for yielding, Harold

bendeth knee to no man. Come, this is
our last meeting." Olaf needed no second
bidding, and with calmness born of cour-
age, coupled with the elation of antici-
pated success, he entered upon the strug-
gle which should end only when one was
victor, the other victim. And now were
savage thrusts, while the hands that but a
fleeting breath before had been clasped in
good fellowship held now within their
grasp the blood-stained keys to the house
of death; back and forth, thrust and
parry, feint, recover, fought these men of
giant souls. Heedless of the fortunes of
the day they flashed steel against steel, but
neither prevailed ; each had drawn blood,
each had found his antagonist as lusty in
action as he had been bold in speech ; the
issue was still doubtful, yet neither thought
of suggesting rest — it was a duel to the
death, agreed beforehand, therefore must
end with death, death alone.

Meantime Harold seemed to have for-
gotten the danger of his men, who, broken,
huddled in spiritless groups, seeking
simply to protect themselves from the mur-

derous assaults of Halfjord's victorious
troops.

"The day is won!" in ecstasy exclaimed
Landsvag's king to Erling as they rested a
moment from the slaughter, but just then,
as if in answer to his boast, there arose a
cry that froze the marrow of their bones.

"Treason! Treason!" was the cry that,
taken up by Erling's men, rolled a resist-
less wave of frenzied sound until the silent
hills, roused from their sleepy dreams, in
scornful screams shriek back in the ring-
ing ears of the combatants: "Treason!
Treason!"

Ah! would that man were less a crea-
ture of sordid interests, then would the
world's vocabulary know no such word as
this; a word so foul that uttered leaves
within the mouth of him who uses it the
nauseous taste of earth's sewers.

Yes, "Treason!" was the cry and
rightly, too, for at the moment when it
seemed that Landsvag must prevail Alric
led his entire force into the enemy's lines
and now Erling, his flank unprotected,
found himself beset by both friend and foe.

The two whom we left struggling to-
gether had not heard the awful cry whose
despairing notes yet quivered in the air,
and still they fought. But now, from dif-
ferent quarters of the field, came rushing
to the scene of this most equal combat
Alric, with glaring, vengeful eyes, and
Erling, who, seeing the speeding traitor,
sought to bury his own trusty blade within
that venomous heart; nor were they all, for
over the uneven plain dashed a maddened
horse whose rider, a woman, seemed not
of this life; rushing on in wild fury she
tore her way through the now disordered
ranks shrieking as she flew: "Olaf! oh!
where is Olaf?" A strange race across a
bloody battlefield. The girl was now
ahead, her quick eye had spied out her
lover and on she rushed like a demon,
heedless of the dead and dying spurned,
crushed beneath her horse's hoofs; behind
her with eyes set and glazed in frightful
murderous fury came Alric and after him
with steady purpose and unfaltering gait,
his Nemesis — Erling.

On, on, the girl urged her frantic steed,

shrieking as she rode: "Olaf! Olaf!" but he heard not; nearer, still nearer she drew and at last his ear caught the frenzied words: "Olaf! beware of the traitor Alric!" He heard and recognizing the voice that spoke, turned with a start of surprise just as Harold attacked him afresh. Like a thunderbolt the frightened horse with its crazy burden dashed between the two combatants, the devoted Hilda received in her soft bosom the steel meant for Olaf and reeling fell beneath the grinding hoofs; before Harold or Olaf recovered themselves Alric from behind ran Olaf through, exclaiming: "This for thy thrust!" and almost at the same moment Erling coming up impaled Alric, hissing: "Traitor!"

Weltering in their blood the three lay beneath the horses' hoofs before Harold was fully aware what had transpired; the first sight which met the king's eyes was Erling with bloody blade confronting him. "What is this?" cried Harold. "Hath Halfjord foul assassins who do murder those engaged in equal combat?"

"Nay, King Harold," replied Erling. "Alric, the traitor, hath killed Olaf; Erling did the same for Alric and now holdeth himself ready for thine own purposes.   Let Erling, I pray thee, take Olaf's place before thee."

Harold, apparently oblivious of the battle raging around him, exclaimed : "Olaf dead ?" as though he had not witnessed the tragedy, then, resting his eyes upon the three bleeding bodies he continued: "Yes, dead, and not by Harold's hand. Pierced through foul treachery from behind, with not a chance to save his noble life, he died even as the dog who slew him."

Clenching his fist he turned again to Erling and fiercely asked : "Why let you not yon venomous serpent live that Harold might wreak upon him fitting vengeance for his most dastardly act?"   Erling making no reply the king continued as if speaking to himself : "Through that ghastly rent escaped the knightliest soul which Harold hath yet seen.   Olaf!   Olaf ! foe though you were mine eyes do weep at your untimely end."   Then seeing apparently for

the first time Hilda's corpse he asked :
" The girl ? who is she ? "

"A gentle maiden whom Olaf loved ! "

"What did she here ?"

" I know not, king, whence came the
gentle Hilda nor yet where she had
gathered news of Alric's foul intent, but
as you fought with Olaf, the maiden riding
hotly sought her lover, crying : 'Beware,
Olaf, of Alric, the traitor !' King, she
hath found her lover and her grave."

" Yea," was the passionate reply, " and
Harold's blade freed her pure soul.   Ah !
Harold, Harold, put up thy blade, which,
seeking flesh of man, hath nothing found
save the warm, pulsing breast of a gentle
woman ! Would to Thor before I sheathed
this sword it had drank deep of the life-
blood of the dastard Alric, then might his
blood in part atone for that which now too
deeply dyes this blade ! "

Through the entire action Harold had
borne himself as one to whom Fate's de-
crees had been already revealed ; seeking
but to keep his troth with Olaf he had
given no attention to the details of the

battle, and during the colloquy between Harold and Erling neither had heeded the changing scenes around them, but when Erling, eager to be doing, repeated his request that he might take Olaf's place, the king first glanced approvingly at the brave fellow, then for the first time swept his eye over the field. After a brief survey he rode close to Erling, and, laying a hand kindly upon his shoulder, said, "Nay, noble knight, another time. Halfjord needeth you now. See!"

Erling, looking, saw the troops of Landsvag, demoralized by Alric's defection, flying in disorder from the field, Halfjord himself, with the remnant of his band of picked men, closely pressed by the victorious enemy. Speechless with surprise and admiration at Harold's magnanimity Erling bowed, then wheeled and dashed away to Halfjord's succor, while Harold rode slowly back to camp away from the scene of combat.

The day was lost to Landsvag, and nothing remained but to save from the wreck as much as possible, and to this end

Halfjord, Jorg and Erling bent all their efforts.   At first the pursuit was sharp, but as the routed army entered the hills they were less closely followed, and by night-fall had reached a place of comparative security, where the weary, disheartened, broken ranks threw themselves upon the dew-bathed grass to seek in friendly sleep forgetfulness of their disgrace.

Halfjord, Jorg and Erling were together, the latter telling of Olaf's death, when the faithful old general, with tears in his eyes, exclaimed, "Ah! would I might have found that blessed sleep which now closeth Olaf's eyes!   Would I had not lived to see Landsvag's humiliation!"

"Even so feel I, good Jorg," was the king's answer, "but there remaineth much for us."

"What would you, king?"

"Save Landsvag."

"Halfjord," gloomily replied the old man, "Jorg's sword is thine, and I do even hope to lay down my life since, seeing that we have lost Olaf and half our army, Landsvag is doomed."

"Not so, Jorg, we will even yet over-
come this Harold."

"King, Jorg is old enough to be thy
father. Jorg telleth thee no son of thine
shall ever sit upon the throne of Landsvag,
nor shalt thou die its king."

"Methinks, good Jorg, the day's disasters
have overcome your sense. Yea, we have
greatly suffered, but Landsvag yet re-
maineth true to her king, and will fight
for him, even though Harold brought
legions upon legions. Halfjord feareth
not Harold, but if that you say be true
what then, Jorg ? What should Halfjord
do ?"

"Make peace, oh ! king, with this thy
enemy, before it were too late."

"He is a most generous foe, king, and
now would exact no terms dishonorable to
thyself or thy people," broke in Erling
eagerly.

"What !" exclaimed Halfjord, "do Jorg
and Erling ask the King of Landsvag to
go on bended knee in suit for peace unto
this knave, who cometh from the south
seeking that which is not his own ? Nay,

my gorge rises at the thought. Let Harold have that he taketh, even though it be all Landsvag, but that which he taketh not Halfjord will keep, and every step he taketh on this our land shall be marked with blood of his slain !" This defiant declaration of their defeated king, the death-knell not of themselves alone—that were of small moment—but of the land of their birth as well, was received with dismay ; but before either could speak an officer approached, escorting a party of mounted men. These proved to be messengers from Harold, bearing with them the corpses of Olaf and Hilda, together with a message of condolence and regret from Halfjord's knightly foe. The king, dismissing the messengers with a suitable reply, ordered the bodies borne to his own castle for interment, and, left alone, murmured : "Olaf said true, this Harold hath a great and noble heart, and yet that maketh him but a more dangerous foe."

CHAPTER IX

Though this is called the legend of Half-
jord the death of the gallant Olaf leaves
but little to tell.

Grunhilde, apprised of the arrival of the
messengers bearing the two bodies, re-
turned at once to Halfjord's castle. Olaf's
tragic death overwhelmed her with sorrow,
but in the rush of events, her consternation
at Landsvag's defeat and the daily reports
of continued successes on Harold's part, she
had no time to indulge her grief. The
full story of the tragedy in which the two
young lovers had died almost in each
other's arms had not been told her and
the part that Alric had played was known
to neither herself nor Olga.

Grunhilde had, for the sake of Hilda
and her message just before she went on
her ride of death, pardoned and restored
to a semblance of old-time favor the maid

Olga, while the latter, though feeling a twinge of conscience whenever she thought of sweet Hilda's rude death, did not yet know the cost to Landsvag of her silence, and felt rather a sense of relief that she had spoken even so late.

Thoroughly aroused, Grunhilde sought in every way to aid her king, scouring the country for recruits and even arming and sending to the front the menials of her household, but it was of no avail. It had been written in the Book of Fate that Landsvag should fall and daily, almost hourly, Harold drove the devoted remnant which still clung to the declining fortunes of their king further and further into the interior. Halfjord, upon whom Olaf's mantle seemed to have fallen, was now a king, a kingly king, most worthy of that crown fast slipping from his head. Halfjord! Halfjord! it is now too late; those squandered hours when Pleasure's wanton smile lured you from the rugged path of duty, and servile sycophants dulled your ears to Olaf's warnings — those hours, marshalled now before your retrospective gaze, seem as the hosts of dead which lie putrefying on a score of fields, hosts you might have saved had you but saved the hours. A king now, Halfjord, but what were you before ? Hardly the lowest serf in your kingdom gave less thought to life's grave responsibilities than did you. This your retribution and in proportion to your discarded duties shall its terrors accumulate !

At last the torn and tattered ravelings of the army that had so proudly gone forth limped wearily, woefully, through the gate of the king's own castle — Landsvag's last stronghold — and there prepared themselves for the siege whose end was inevitable. Harold came and like a mighty serpent his army wound its crushing folds around the frowning walls.

Jorg and Erling were still among the living, though each had most frantically sought death's sweet release from impending humiliation. The queen, hearing that Erling was present at Olaf's death, questioned him and then heard for the first time the full story of Alric's treachery and murder. The story was told before Olga

—Olga, whose one word spoken in season might have changed the course of history —and when Erling had gone, the queen, with a withering smile, said to the girl who with cheeks as pale as death's phantom steed sat like a piece of stone : "You are both murderess and traitress!" Olga rose and left the chamber. That night the sleeping inmates of the castle were aroused by an agonized shriek, followed quickly by a heavy fall, and in the morning the mangled remains of the unhappy Olga were found beneath her window.

My story draws to a close ; already I have, in seeking to drive away the ennui of these tedious hours, spun it out to a length discouraging to the possible reader. Reader ? An odd conceit, that these pages will ever find their way to my fellow-men, and yet I hope even against hope.

What need to recount the privations, the sufferings, of the beleaguered garrison, the sorties of the desperate, starving men, the repulsed assaults of the besiegers, who, like a great flock of buzzards watching the dying throes of a helpless lion, not content with the slow approach of dissolution, sought to hasten death with their sharp, tearing talons? The history of one prolonged siege is, barring details, the history of them all—Halfjord capitulated. How could it be otherwise? Harold, filled with admiration of his brave foe, with his usual magnanimity accepted the surrender, leaving the terms open to be settled afterward as between kings.

On the day when the gates were to be opened Jorg, emaciated, starving, hardly able to stand erect, weeping like a baby, said to Halfjord: "Fate hath been kind to many—the princely Olaf, mine own gallant Jegge, last of our race, and countless thousands of others have, through the friendly shafts of our foes, pillowed their noble heads upon the soft bosom of this their native land, but Jorg, who for a lifetime hath borne weapons for Landsvag nor ever yet before hath bended knee to foe — Jorg, who should have died before, must needs behold an alien in the seat of Landsvag's king. Ah! Halfjord! Halfjord! why died we not at birth ? Great Odin !

Let the kindly curtain of eternal blindness roll its grateful clouds before old Jorg's despairing eyes, that I may not behold the desecration of this day !"

Halfjord made no reply — with tortured soul whose festering wounds had poisoned all the springs of life, with a heroism born of a kingly heart he sought to bear himself with a most kingly mien through the ordeal before him and in such a mood it is not safe for man, however colossal his soul, to trust himself to words—treacherous words, in their very forming a tremor of the lip, a quaver of the voice, betrays the grinding agony which the giant soul may, through a silent smile, hide from the prying world.

The hour arrived. Halfjord, Jorg and Erling, with a handful of trusty followers, stood, almost tottering in their weakness, awaiting the signal that, sounding triumph to those without, meant desolation to those within. Harold's great army, full of lusty pride, was marshaled in grand array upon the surrounding plains; the trumpet sounded, trembling, gray-haired veterans threw open those gates that had so faithfully resisted armed foes without but to yield to that most insidious foe within — starvation — and through the open portal rode, not a great host to gloat over the dying struggles of the once mighty Landsvag, but a single horseman, the knightly Harold himself alone.

Dismounting in the court-yard Harold advanced to the king who was now his prisoner, saying : "Halfjord, thou hast nobly defended thyself, and while we do rejoice at this our great success yet do we grieve with thee over thy downfall and even more over the death of the gallant Olaf, whom we did love as brother while we battled with him as a foe."

Halfjord was not prepared for such kindness ; despite himself his eyes filled with tears as he replied : "Harold, thou art kind unto one who now yields himself thy prisoner."

"Not so, good Halfjord," was the response. "Pluck up thy spirits, thou art neither foe nor prisoner now, but Harold's friend and vassal. We would have thee govern for us this thy goodly land and Harold can sleep easy on his couch with Landsvag beneath thy true eye."

Harold had extended his hand as he spoke — Halfjord took the proffered hand and these two kings, the victor and the vanquished, gazed into each other's eyes; at last, in tones whose determination left no room for argument, while through them ran a note of sadness, Halfjord spoke: "I thank thee, king, but it may not be; Halfjord will not rule as vassal where once he was king."

Disappointment and admiration were blended in the look which Harold bent upon him as he said: "Thine was a king's answer, and its spirit pleases us. We would fain have thee with us, yet will we not force thee; thou shalt have thy wish, brave Halfjord. What wilt thou?"

"Oh! king, thou art generous unto thy fallen foe. Halfjord would take ship and go far from hence, for his eyes weep tears of blood at sight of the desolation of his land."

"It shall be as thou desirest, Halfjord," was the quiet reply, at which the unfor-

tunate king, clasping Harold about the
neck, exclaimed: "Verily, thou art a
king!"

"And you, noble Jorg?" asked Harold,
as, disengaging himself from Halfjord, he
extended a hand to the old man.

"King," answered the faithful follower,
"see, Jorg's hair is white with the snows of
many winters; I am too old to learn how
to serve a new master; I go with my
king."

"You have a true and loyal heart. With
such men as these I marvel not, Halfjord,
that thou hast so long withstood Harold,
And you, brave knight, who would have
taken Olaf's place against Harold himself,
what say you?"

"Harold, Erling also goeth with his
king."

"Harold is now your king."

"Not so, Harold, thou hast conquered,
but Halfjord is still Landsvag's king, even
though thou hast wrested from him his fair
crown."

"Well said, brave Erling. Halfjord, I
would I had an hundred such men, men

who desert not when fortune frowns. And these thy brave followers?" waving his hand at the men who had stood silently at arms behind their king. A cry arose as if from one throat: "We cast our lot with Halfjord!"

Harold, deeply impressed with the inflexible loyalty of the entire garrison, said: ' It is well. Thou mayest depart with thy followers, Halfjord. I leave thee in possession here until thou art prepared, nor shall the presence of aliens in this, thy home, disturb thy last hours here." Then saluting in turn each of the three men he said to the dethroned king: "Halfjord, thou art a king and deservest a better fate." To Jorg and Erling: "My heart yearneth for such followers as ye men of Landsvag." Then mounted and rode away.

Not long after his departure a train of provisions sent by Harold to the famishing garrison entered the castle.

Some two days were consumed in preparations, and on the third day the little troop filed out, taking their way toward the distant seashore. True to his promise, Harold not only refrained from taking possession of the castle during Halfjord's occupancy, but, with refined consideration, so disposed his force that when the mournful train of self-expatriated exiles passed with tear-dimmed eyes they were spared the humiliation of marching under the eyes of the victors. .

We see no more of noble Harold and but little more of Halfjord, since it were a weary task to follow these wanderers through the trials, sufferings, privations of their journey. Taking ship the followers of Halfjord, some two hundred souls, set sail for far-away Iceland, but adverse winds drove them from their course ; they were lost on the pathless ocean. During the time that they sought in vain to recover their course the queen, Grunhilde, after giving birth to a son, whom she named Olaf, yielded up her life, and her body was consigned to the soft caresses of the rolling waves.

At last they sighted land, but, owing to the ice, were unable to approach it close

enough to determine if it was inhabited or
habitable. (I have every reason to assume
that this land was Greenland.) For days they
skirted this frowning, ice-locked coast,
until finally they again entered open water,
and there found a current that bore them
resistlessly northward. Death in a thou-
sand ways now staring them in the face,
they lost heart, but the noble Halfjord
sought in every possible way to revive
their drooping spirits, succeeding in rous-
ing them to one last effort. Finally land
was again sighted, and this time without
the menacing fringe of ice. The current
bore them close in shore ; they anchored,
landing, I should judge, not far from the
spot where my ship of ice stranded, and
there the good King Halfjord founded the
city of Nikiva.

Halfjord reigned many years, claiming
toward the end of his life to have the gift
of prophecy, and telling his people that
he should return hereafter and lead them
to recover the kingdom Harold had
wrested from them. They believed him,
and to this day have looked for his return,

hence their welcome to me, though since the ships in which they came have long since rotted, and they have neither material nor practical knowledge for fashioning or handling others, it is to me a matter of much speculation how they expect me to lead them from this place — a matter of much concern to me, though apparently of none to them.

This, then, is the legend of Halfjord as told in Nikiva, and to the minds of this people their legend suggests but two ideas — the ultimate return of their beloved King Halfjord and the treachery of Alric the Bloody-haired—treachery so foul that after a lapse of ten centuries the taint of its curse still hangs around, working frightful death to the unfortunate babe who enters the world with locks that suggest the "Bloody Hair."

www.ingramcontent.com/pod-product-compliance
Lightning Source LLC
Chambersburg PA
CBHW020350030726
47496CB00007B/2083